Workshop on Computational Semantics Beyond Events and Roles (SemBEaR 2017)

Valencia, Spain
4 April 2017

ISBN: 978-1-5108-3869-7

Preface

During the last decade, semantic representation of text has focused on extracting propositional meaning, i.e., capturing who does what to whom, how, when and where. Several corpora are available, and existing tools extract this kind of knowledge, e.g., role labelers trained on PropBank or NomBank. Nevertheless, most current representations tend to disregard significant meaning encoded in human language. For example, sentences 1-2 below share the same argument structure regarding verb contracted, but do not convey the same overall meaning. While in the first example John contracting the disease is factual, in the second it is not:

1. John likely contracted the disease when a mouse bit him in the Adirondacks.
2. John never contracted the disease although a mouse bit him in the Adirondacks.

In order to truly capture what these sentences mean, aspects of meaning that go beyond identifying events and their roles (e.g., uncertainty, negation and attribution) must be taken into account. The Workshop on Computational Semantics Beyond Events and Roles focuses on a broad range of semantic phenomena that lays beyond the identification and linking of eventualities and their semantic arguments with relations such as *agent* (who), *theme* (what) and *location* (where), here so called SemBEaR.

SemBEaR is pervasive in human language and, while studied from a theoretical perspective, computational models are still scarce. Humans use language to describe events that do not correlate with a real situation in the world. They express desires, intentions and plans, and also discuss events that did not happen or are unlikely to happen. Events are often described hypothetically, and speculation can be used to explain why something is a certain way without a strong commitment. Humans do not always (want to) tell the (whole) truth: they may use deception to hide lies. Devices such as irony and sarcasm are employed to play with words so that what is said is not what is meant. Finally, humans not only describe their personal views or experiences, but also attribute statements to others. These phenomena are not exclusive of opinionated texts. They are ubiquitous in language, including scientific works and news as exemplified below:

- Female leaders might have avoided world wars.
- Political experts speculate that Donald Trump's meltdown is beginning.
- Infected people typically don't become contagious until they develop symptoms.
- Medical personnel can be infected if they don't use protective gear, such as surgical masks and gloves.
- You can only catch Ebola from coming into direct contact with the bodily fluids of someone who has the disease and is showing symptoms.
- We have never seen a human virus change the way it is transmitted.
- The government did not release the files until 1998.

In its 2017 edition, the Workshop on Computational Semantics Beyond Events and Roles (SemBEaR) brought together scientists working on these kind of semantic phenomena within computational semantics. The workshop was collocated with the 15th Conference of the European Chapter of the Association for Computational Linguistics (EACL 2017) in Valencia, Spain, and took place on April 4, 2017. The program consisted of oral presentations and an invited talk by Johan Bos (University of Groningen, Netherlands). SemBEaR 2017 is a follow-up of four previous events: the 2010 Negation and Speculation in Natural Language Processing Workshop (NeSp-NLP 2010), and the Extra-Propositional Aspects of Meaning (ExProM) in Computational Linguistics Workshops held in 2012, 2015 and 2016.

We would like to thank the authors of papers for their interesting contributions, the members of the program committee for their insightful reviews, and Johan Bos for being the invited speaker. We are also grateful to the National Science Foundation for a grant to support student travel to the workshop.

Eduardo Blanco, University of North Texas
Roser Morante, VU University Amsterdam
Roser Saurí, Oxford University Press
Workshop Co-Chairs

Table of Contents

This page intentionally left blank.

Workshop Program

Tuesday April 4, 2017

9:20–9:30   Opening Remarks

9:30–10:00   *Understanding the Semantics of Narratives of Interpersonal Violence through Reader Annotations and Physiological Reactions*
Alexander Calderwood, Elizabeth A. Pruett, Raymond Ptucha, Christopher Homan and Cecilia Ovesdotter Alm

10:00–10:20   *Intension, Attitude, and Tense Annotation in a High-Fidelity Semantic Representation*
Gene Kim and Lenhart Schubert

10:20–10:40   *Towards a lexicon of event-selecting predicates for a French FactBank*
Ingrid Falk and Fabienne Martin

10:40–11:00   Discussion Session 1

11:00–11:30   Coffee Break

11:30–12:00   *Universal Dependencies to Logical Form with Negation Scope*
Federico Fancellu, Siva Reddy, Adam Lopez and Bonnie Webber

    Invited talk
12:00–13:00   *Meaning Banking beyond Events and Roles*
Johan Bos

13:00–14:30   Lunch

14:30–15:00   *The Scope and Focus of Negation: A Complete Annotation Framework for Italian*
Begoña Altuna, Anne-Lyse Minard and Manuela Speranza

15:00–15:30   *Annotation of negation in the IULA Spanish Clinical Record Corpus*
Montserrat Marimon, Jorge Vivaldi and Núria Bel

15:30–15:50   *Annotating Negation in Spanish Clinical Texts*
Noa Cruz, Roser Morante, Manuel J. Maña López, Jacinto Mata Vázquez and Carlos L. Parra Calderón

15:50–16:00   Discussion Session 2

16:00–16:30   Coffee Break

16:30–16:50   *Neural Networks for Negation Cue Detection in Chinese*
Hangfeng He, Federico Fancellu and Bonnie Webber

16:50–17:10   *An open-source tool for negation detection: a maximum-margin approach*
Martine Enger, Erik Velldal and Lilja Øvrelid

17:10–18:00   Discussion Session 3

Understanding the Semantics of Narratives of Interpersonal Violence through Reader Annotations and Physiological Reactions

Alexander Calderwood[1], Elizabeth A. Pruett[2],
Raymond Ptucha[3], Christopher M. Homan[3] and Cecilia O. Alm[3]

[1]Montana State University
[2]University of South Carolina
[3]Rochester Institute of Technology
[1]`alexander.d.calderwood@gmail.com`
[2]`pruette95@gmail.com`
[3]`{rwpeec,cmhvcs,coagla}@rit.edu`

Abstract

Interpersonal violence (IPV) is a prominent sociological problem that affects people of all demographic backgrounds. By analyzing how readers interpret, perceive, and react to experiences narrated in social media posts, we explore an understudied source for discourse about abuse. We asked readers to annotate Reddit posts about relationships with vs. without IPV for stakeholder roles and emotion, while measuring their galvanic skin response (GSR), pulse, and facial expression. We map annotations to coreference resolution output to obtain a labeled coreference chain for stakeholders in texts, and apply automated semantic role labeling for analyzing IPV discourse. Findings provide insights into how readers process roles and emotion in narratives. For example, abusers tend to be linked with violent actions and certain affect states. We train classifiers to predict stakeholder categories of coreference chains. We also find that subjects' GSR noticeably changed for IPV texts, suggesting that co-collected measurement-based data about annotators can be used to support text annotation.

1 Introduction

More than one in three women and one in four men in the United States have experienced rape, physical violence, and/or stalking by an intimate partner (Black et al., 2011). One in nine girls and one in 53 boys under the age of eighteen are sexually abused by an adult (Finkelhor et al., 2014). Additionally,

Figure 1: Experiment setup. Subjects read texts and completed annotation tasks while sensors captured their pulse and GSR and video-recorded their faces and upper bodies.

approximately one in ten elders in the USA have faced intimidation, isolation, neglect, and threats of violence.[1]

Such *interpersonal violence* (IPV)[2] can lead to injury, depression, post-traumatic stress disorder, substance abuse, sexually transmitted diseases, as well as hospitalization, disability, or death (Black et al., 2011). Most of the science on IPV is based on survey and interview data. However, the nature of IPV relationships can make people feel uncomfortable or unsafe when participating in such studies, leading to inaccurate results. Also, surveys can be costly and time-consuming to carry out (Schrading et al., 2015b).

Social media is an understudied source of IPV data. Over 79% of adults that frequent the internet

---

[1]https://www.ncoa.org/public-policy-action/elder-justice/elder-abuse-facts/

[2]For the purposes of this study, we use the WHO definition of IPV, while we recognize that the acronym commonly refers to "Intimate Partner Violence", a subset of this phenomenon.

Proceedings of the Workshop Computational Semantics Beyond Events and Roles (SemBEaR), pages 1–9,
Valencia, Spain, April 4, 2017. ©2017 Association for Computational Linguistics

utilize social media (Greenwood et al., 2016). Online, individuals can anonymously share their experiences without fear of embarrassment or repercussions. Such narratives can also provide more details than surveys, and may lead to a deeper understanding of IPV. Nonetheless, it is extremely difficult to establish reference annotations useful for predictive modeling for discourse topics as emotionally charged as IPV.

We meet these challenges with a combination of annotator labeling, analyzing annotations, applying semantic processing techniques (coreference resolution, semantic role labeling, sentiment analysis), developing classifiers, and studying physiological sensor measurements collected in real-time from annotators as they read and annotate texts. Our contributions include:

1. Studying characteristics of the key players and their actions in IPV narratives.

2. Using coreference chains as units that map human to automated annotations for analyzing semantic roles, predicates, and characteristics such as pronoun usage to affective tone.

3. Applying distinct semantic features for classifying stakeholders, using coreference chains as classification units.

4. Analyzing how annotators interpret emotional tone of texts vs. their own reactions to them, and discussing the link to annotators' measurement-based sensor data gathered as they labeled texts about abuse.

2   Background and Related Work

The World Health Organization (WHO) includes in its definition of IPV acts committed by family members and intimate partners, as well as those who are unrelated to or unfamiliar with the victim (Krug et al., 2002). It divides violence into physical, sexual, psychological, and deprivational/neglect categories. The Duluth model provides another established categorization of types of violence, but was originally developed for therapy treating men who abuse women, rather than for understanding IPV scientifically (Rizza, 2009). Our study takes as its theoretical basis categories from the Department of Justice: physical, sexual, emotional, economic and psychological.[3]   This

---

[3] https://www.justice.gov/ovw/domestic-violence

categorization most faithfully captures our studied narratives.

Schrading et al. (2015a) developed classifiers to determine whether a Reddit post described abuse. In the study, the subreddit to which the post belonged was used to map to binary gold-standard labels: if a post came from a subreddit such as */r/survivorsofabuse*, it was categorized as a post about abuse. We also draw upon such social media text data as a basis for our study, as Reddit allows us to consider narrative texts. However, we consider human perception and text annotation in conjunction with biophysical data sensed from reader-annotators.

Our study makes use of coreference resolution and semantic role labeling (SRL); the former to identify mentions linked to the same referent which are semantically co-indexed, while the latter identifies the relationships of predicates and their arguments in sentences. For example, SRL maps *entity causing damage* and *agent* as semantic descriptions of *he* in *he hurt me*. For IPV texts, current automated SRL does not directly correspond to IPV researchers' characterization frameworks, but automatically processing IPV-related texts in meaningful ways could enable IPV researchers to take advantage of such tools.

We use *Linguistic Inquiry and Word Count (LIWC)*, a resource that cross-references word tokens with dictionaries containing categories of words such as positive/negative emotion and first/second/third person (Tausczik and Pennebaker, 2010). Normalizing the frequencies with which words occur in each category dictionary by the length of the input text allows for observations of lexical trends.

This study also considers physiological responses of reader-annotators when collecting annotations. Pulse changes have been associated with emotional reactions, as has galvanic skin response (GSR) with, for instance, arousal and stress. Prior work reports on observed changes in GSR when drivers navigated through various routes, noting spikes in skin conductance at particularly stressful traffic points (Taylor, 1964). More recently, researchers showed that GSR readings changed when individuals completed tasks with increased cognitive load (Shi et al., 2007). We incorporate forms of affect assessment and self-reporting in order to examine both reported and sensor data.

1:Partner-A [1/1]
2:Partner-B [1/1]
3:Secondary
4:Other [2/2]
5:Text-emotion [1/1]
6:My-emotion [1/1]

1. Identify if any of the stakeholders to the left are mentioned in the text. If so, indicate their first occurrence in the text. Some may not occur at all, or the same label could apply to more than one person:

"My former employer called and wants me back! I left my employer about three weeks ago because I was unhappy (no recognition, no mentoring/training, and I shared different values/ethics than the other managers did). Yesterday, their corporate office called me out of the blue and asked me to consider a promotion to their headquarters. The woman (someone very high up that I respect a lot) told me that she and other corporate employees were bummed to hear I had left, and considered me to be very talented and awesome.

Figure 2: Subjects completed reading and annotation tasks with the eHOST annotation software.

3 Annotation Experiment and Pre-Processing

We selected 80 narrative posts from relevant subreddits, such as */r/relationship_advice* and */r/survivorsofabuse*. 40 texts were about relationships[4] with IPV and 40 control texts were about relationships without IPV mentions. Texts presented to subjects, often from anonymous 'throwaway' accounts, contained no personal details.

Twenty subjects read and annotated texts using eHOST[5], while sensors recorded pulse, GSR, and facial reactions (see Figures 1 and 2). Subjects were college-aged adults (10 women, 9 men, 1 non-disclose). They received $20 for participating.

Subjects completed two trials, each lasting 25 minutes; Trial 1 without IPV and Trial 2 with IPV. The ordering of the trials was consistent across participants, while texts within each trial were presented in random order. Time was extended an extra five minutes for one participant.

For each text, the tasks were:

1. *Indicate the first occurrence of each stakeholder in the text.*
   Labels for Trial 1: Partner, Secondary, and Other. Labels for Trial 2: Victim, Abuser, Victim-Supporter, Abuse-Enabler, and Other. Labels could apply to multiple stakeholders in a text.

2. *What is the dominant emotion conveyed in the text?*
   Subjects selected 1 of 8 possible choices from the Plutchik wheel of emotions: Anger, Fear, Anticipation, Trust, Surprise, Sadness, Joy, or Disgust (Plutchik, 2001).

3. *How do you feel reading this text?*
   Subjects indicated their own emotional response to each text.

4. *Which types of abuse does this account fall under?*
   For texts with IPV, subjects indicated the types of violence mentioned in each text: Physical, Sexual, Emotional, Psychological, and Economic.

In the two trials (reading and annotating texts with vs. without IPV), we recorded subjects' physiological responses. Specifically, a Shimmer 3 GSR+ sensor recorded pulse and GSR on their non-dominant hands, while Camtasia[6] recorded subjects' faces and upper bodies and their screens (see Figure 1).

3.1 Linguistic Data Processing

In order to cover more texts and minimize boredom and fatigue, we asked subjects to label only the first mention of each stakeholder in each text. *Coreference resolution* identifies multiple references to the same individual in a given text; for example, *my father*, *he*, and *dad* might refer to the same individual that together form a disambiguated coreference chain. Automatic coreference resolvers such as CoreNLP[7] are reasonably accurate (Manning et al., 2014). We used CoreNLP to collect the remaining mentions of these stakeholders. Then, we manually inspected and corrected coreference linkages; one issue addressed was falsely non-linked chains.

Stakeholder labels assigned by subjects were associated with their coreference chain by use of an algorithm that took into account the similarity between these two labeled sets of text. This algorithm minimized the Levenshtein distance between words contained in the subject-labeled text and the coreference text, placing a higher weight on matching noun/pronoun headwords. Then, each chain was assigned an aggregate stakeholder

---

[4] Here a *relationship* is an ongoing dynamic between any two parties. This allows analysis to consider parent/child relationships as well as non-familial relationships such as employee/employer.

[5] http://ehostdoc.com

[6] https://www.techsmith.com/camtasia.html

[7] http://stanfordnlp.github.io/CoreNLP/

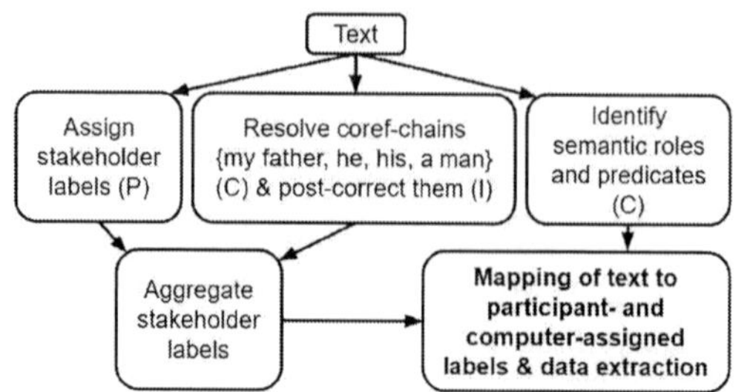

Figure 3: Diagram of data processing pipeline (P = reader-participant, I = investigator, C = computer-based processing).

label based on the label most frequently assigned to it.

Next, each text was run through the Illinois Semantic Role Labeler, part of the Illinois Curator package of NLP tools (Punyakanok et al., 2008). We considered the assigned text labels of (verb) predicates and of the following arguments linked to them: A0, typically the subject, and A1, typically the (direct) object. As an example, given the sentence *He protected his brother*, for the predicate *protect*, the A0 *he* may be labeled *protector* and A1 *brother* labeled *protected*. The same algorithm that was used to find the coreference chain associated with a given reader's annotation text was used to automatically associate the semantic role nodes with their coreference chain.

Figure 3 shows the entire mapping framework. Once complete, each coreference chain contained: (1) all human-assigned stakeholder labels, (2) the aggregate human-assigned stakeholder label (the most frequently assigned stakeholder), and (3) all semantic labels assigned to it that were generated by the SRL tool. We did not manually correct the SRL-generated labels.

This allows for examination of trends between the human-assigned stakeholder labels and the SRL-generated text labels. Matching also enabled the use of SRL features for stakeholder classification.

3.2 Physiological Sensor Data Processing

Multimodal results were synchronized by the system clock, also used as a reference to know when subjects encountered each text in the trials. The Consensys software of the Shimmer 3 GSR+ sensor was used to process and export the GSR and pulse data with timestamps that were subsequently synchronized with the Camtasia timestamps. We

used Affectiva[8] to infer the emotional expression from subjects' video-recorded faces.

Facial expression data and two forms of emotion annotation pertain to 20 subjects, while the pulse and GSR sensor data comprises 18 subjects. For two subjects, the Shimmer 3 GSR+ sensor was not configured properly and thus discarded.

Occasional missing values or spikes in sensor readings, caused by brief hand movements which disrupted the sensor, necessitated filtering the data. Erroneous readings were detected by high frequency deviation from neighbors and replaced with neighborhood values. A Gaussian filter smoothed the GSR and pulse data. From there, we calculated the average GSR and pulse per text per participant. GSR, when measured in KOhms, decreases during periods of stress or arousal as skin conductivity increases. In order to compare results across subjects, all GSR data was normalized using feature standardization.

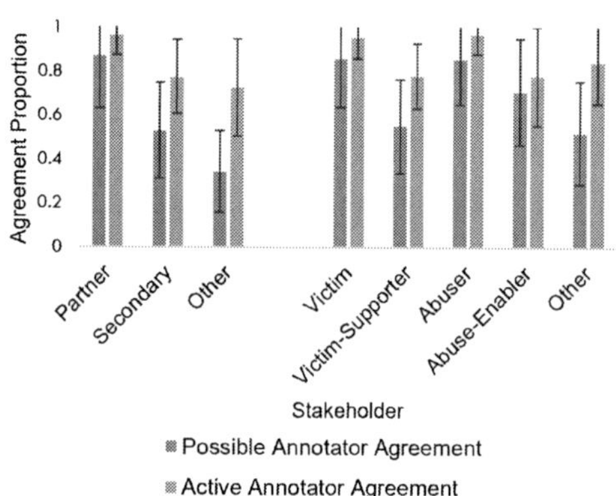

Figure 4: The proportion of agreement between annotators about stakeholder labels regarding the same coreference chain. Agreement was high, and especially for Victim, Abuser, and Partner.

4 Results of Linguistic Analysis

Annotations. On average, the texts about relationships without IPV contained two Partners, while texts with IPV contained one Victim and one Abuser. Subjects demonstrated a high degree of agreement for assigning most stakeholder labels, as shown in Figure 4. Since every subject did not annotate all possible coreference chains for a given text, two measures of agreement are given: possible annotator agreement refers to the proportion of agreement between all participants who annotated

---

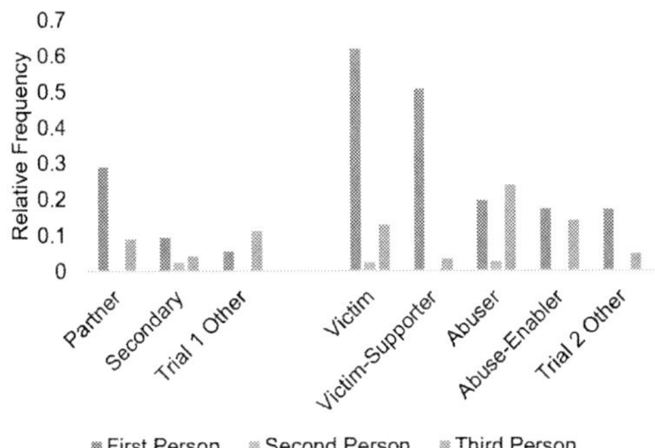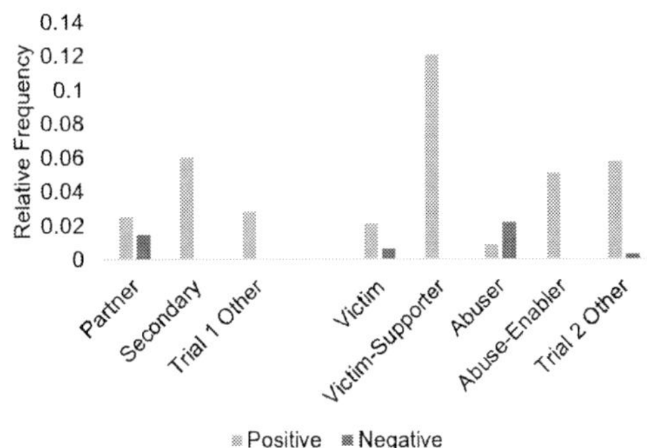

Figure 5: Relative frequency of point-of-view words by stakeholder label. A first-person perspective was strongly associated with Victim and Victim-Supporter stakeholders. For Abuser, a third-person perspective dominated.

Figure 6: Relative frequency of words linked to positive/negative emotion by stakeholder. Victim-Supporter had most positive lexical affinity vs. Abuser for negative.

the text, while active annotator agreement ignores participants who did not mark any stakeholder category in the coreference chain in question.

LIWC Results. Many Victim and Victim-Supporter coreference chains associated strongly with first person, while Abuser was one of few stakeholders with more third person association; see Figure 5.

Emotion lexicon appeared scarce within stakeholder coreference chains, with the notable exception of the Anger category in Abuser coreference chains. Anxiety was absent, and Sadness was present only in Partner coreference chains. However, sentiment dimensions, with broader positive and negative emotion categories, registered substantial levels of positive lexical affinity for many stakeholders, especially for Victim-Supporter, as demonstrated in Figure 6, but also for Abuser-Enabler. Again, Abusers are one of few stakeholders with observable negative diction; Partners rate second. We note that not all IPV-free texts were necessarily positive, but rather did not contain violence. As another note, only the text within coreference chains was considered in the LIWC analysis, necessitating careful interpretation of these results.

SRL Results. Tables 1 and 2 demonstrate the top labels assigned by the SRL system to coreference chains marked as Abusers and Victims. Abuser stakeholders occur more frequently in the A0 category, while Victim stakeholders occur more frequently in the A1 category. To produce these tables, the labels appearing frequently in Victim or Abuser coreferences that also appear frequently in Partner coreference chains have not been reported, so as to remove labels that do not pertain specifically to IPV. Our motivation is to highlight the differences between SRL text labels generated for Victim and Abuser categories, so labels appearing also for Partner, such as *topic*, or *thing done*, can here be discarded for sake of comparison.

The SRL-generated text labels make intuitive sense when compared with their human-annotated stakeholder coreference chains. For example, Abuser stakeholders involve *controller, entity making a threat*, and even *abuser*, suggesting that a mapping to an Abuser coarse-grained label seems possible. Similarly, predicate text labels such as *hit, threaten*, and *control* that appear when the Abuser is the doer clearly point to violent behaviors, while the the predicate texts associated with Victim as A1 are indicative of violence being inflicted on the individual.

The set of labels given to these stakeholders is not disjoint from one another (exemplified by the need to stoplist Partner labels from Abuser/Victim labels as discussed above). The SRL occasionally assigned *abuser* to a stakeholder marked by the human annotators as Victim. Classifiers may still need more features than semantic role labels alone in order to reach high precision.

Stakeholder Classification. Simple features extracted from coreference texts were passed into several classification engines to see if accurate stakeholder label predictions could be made.

Abuser A0 (57)	abuser, agent; agent, hitter - animate only!; entity making a threat...; screamer; assumer of attribute; controller; allower; sender; operator; causer of assurance; rememberer; advisor; causer of dependence...; persuasive entity, agent; killer; possession; puller, agent; provider; entity doing the dropping; tolerator; observer; air; acceptor, pursuer
Victim A1 (74)	corpse; thing hit; entity abused; entity experiencing hurt...; thing wanted; subject; thing thrown; entity respected; stock; victim; apologize for; thing sitting; thing taken; thing destroyed; protected; impelled person; thing trembling; thing; impelled agent; patient, entity pleased; thing standing; thing flying; squozen

Table 1: Most frequent SRL-assigned text labels (in descending order) for Abuser as A0 and Victim as A1.

Partner	be; know; do; get; want; have; say; come; see; feel; think; tell; need; see; go; start; help; talk; make; go; find; do; help;
Abuser A0	abuse; hit; threaten; treat; send; control; scream; provide; coerce; belong; follow; calm; tolerate; accuse; disagree; insist; change; drop; counsel; cut; run; walk; lock;
Victim A1	kill; hit; abuse; hurt; want; depress; talk; respect; rape; marry; slam; accuse; feel; apologize; ignore; attack; sign; coerce; protect; rob; endure; throw; fall

Table 2: Top labels (in descending order) assigned to predicates when Abuser is the A0 argument, and Victim is the A1 argument, after discarding overlapping Partner A0/A1 predicates. The occurrence of predicates of violence for Abuser and Victim as subject vs. object is striking. Other themes include cognitive manipulation and affect.

Stakeholder labels from Trial 1 and Trial 2, with the Other label from both trials grouped together, formed seven classes. Features extracted based on the coreference chains included their A0 and A1 text labels, their A0 and A1 predicate text labels, their text's unigrams, and their LIWC frequency counts.

The unigram feature was stoplisted and lemmatized, and text features were limited to the top 50 most common words/labels. The best performing model was an ensemble of 10 random forest bagged trees. Unigrams alone yield 33.5% k-fold classification accuracy, and adding the SRL and LIWC features improves to 38.5%. An ablation analysis showed text unigrams, followed by A1 text labels, then LIWC counts, as most valuable, and text labels from A1 predicates, then A0 predicates as least valuable.

5 Results of Physiological and Other Analysis

Reading Time. To avoid fatigue, the time limit was the same for each trial. Because the trial with IPV texts required an extra task (determining types of abuse in the text), subjects covered fewer texts in that trial. On average, participants covered 21.5 texts in the trial without IPV, and 16 texts in the trial with IPV. To explore whether texts about IPV took longer to read, while accounting for the additional task, we adjusted the reading instance duration of the second trial by 25%. Adjusted reading times between the two trials showed no difference in how long it took to read the texts.

Reported Emotions. Subjects reported their subjective opinion on the dominant emotions conveyed in each text, and the emotion they felt for each text. Figure 7 demonstrates several noteworthy differences in the proportions of emotions across texts. When reading texts involving IPV, the proportion reported for texts conveying fear and sadness clearly increased. For the self-reported reader emotions there are also differences between the two trials, as shown in Figure 7. Negative emotions such as sadness, fear, and especially anger increased.

Overall, from the trial without IPV to the trial

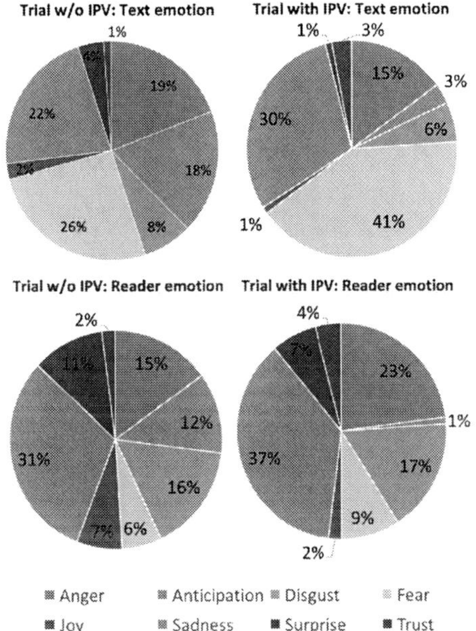

Figure 7: *Top:* Percentage of emotions reported to be text-conveyed per trial. *Bottom:* Percentage of emotions reported to be felt by subjects per trial. From Trial 1 to Trial 2, negative emotions like fear and sadness increased.

with IPV, the proportion of reported emotions like joy and anticipation decreased. In terms of anticipation, texts about relationships without IPV often sought advice about an ongoing dilemma, whereas many texts about relationships with IPV narrated about events in the past. Trust marginally increased for both text-conveyed and self-reported emotions.

Fear was generally more often reported as conveyed by the text than felt by the reader. In contrast, disgust and sadness were more often reported as reader emotions. The findings suggest that for affect-related annotation, it can be useful to collect both text-focused and reader-experienced emotion.

Facial Expressions. Affectiva, an emotion recognition software, analyzes the facial expressions of videos and assesses relative joy, fear, disgust, sadness, anger, surprise, and contempt. For each subject, the Affectiva results were split according to text timestamps, and then the highest ranked emotion was calculated for that text. Affectiva's output displayed surprise, contempt, or disgust for most subjects; the latter two may relate to false positives for unexpressive, stoic faces (such

as from concentrating on reading and annotation), while for the former when participants yawned or opened the mouth widely, Affectiva reported surprise. In general, faces tended to be unexpressive.

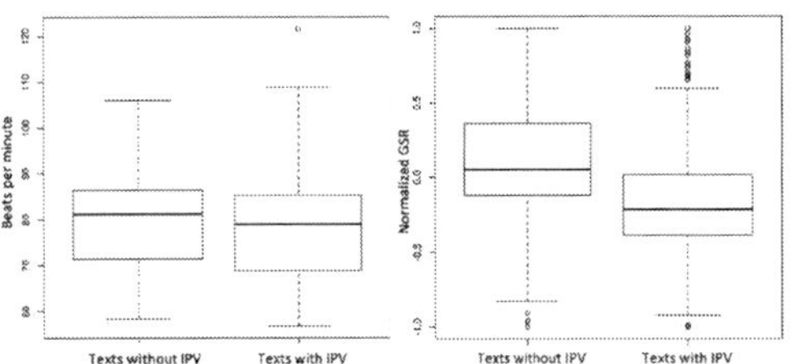

Figure 8: *Left:* Subjects' average pulse per text across trials. IPV trial had slightly lower mean beats per minute and wider variability across subjects. *Right:* Normalized GSR across subjects between trials in KOhms. Most subjects expressed noticeably lower (more prominent) GSR for the IPV trial.

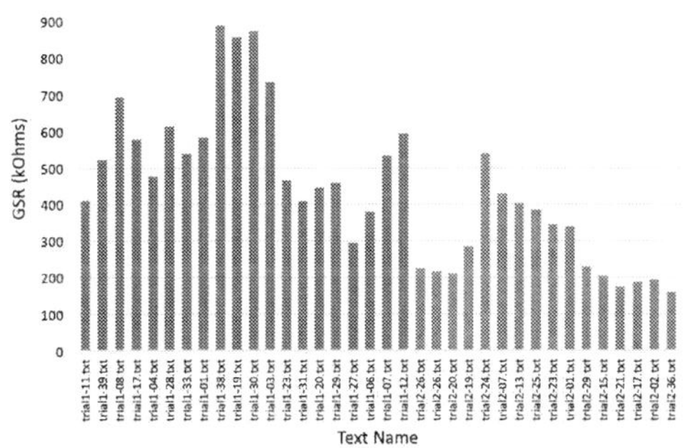

Figure 9: One subjects's average GSR in KOhms, per text. At the first text with IPV (ID: trial2-26), GSR drops. The lower GSR overall for Trial 2 suggests the subject had a stronger physiological reaction to reading texts about IPV. One text occurs twice due to subject looking back at this text during reading-annotation; our analysis included look-back data.

Pulse. Comparing average beats per minute across the trials without and with IPV displayed little change between trials; see Figure 8 (left panel). Across subjects, the mean pulse for reading and annotating texts without IPV was 79.4 beats per minute, and the mean for texts with IPV was 78.0 beats per minute. A histogram of the average pulse per text for each subject was generated in order to examine if certain texts stood out. While single-text spikes in pulse were observed for different subjects, upon review of videos, these rather showed movement (putting on a jacket, coughing and covering mouth) during these texts.

Galvanic Skin Response. GSR data showed noticeably lower KOhms during the trial with IPV for 14 out of 18 participants. KOhms measure the resistance of the skin, so a decrease in resistance indicates higher sweat levels. After normalizing the GSR data, we were able to compare results across subjects. On average, scores decreased when subjects began reading about relationships with violence, and remained low, as shown in Figure 8 (right panel).

One might wonder whether wearing a sensor for a long period of time would cause sweat to accumulate on participants irrespective of the text content. However, for 4 out of 18 participants, the KOhm levels remained approximately the same or increased during the trial with IPV. This suggests that the act of wearing a sensor does not automatically create a sweat response. In addition, the drop in KOhms from the trial without IPV to the trial with IPV was sudden, rather than a gradual decline; see Figure 9.

Physiological Reaction and Annotations. Besides shedding new light on IPV, this study provides an unusual exploration of the correspondence between reader-estimated dominant text/reader emotions and reader physiological reactions. It is interesting that subjects' GSR noticeably changed when reading texts with IPV. As affect annotation usually is a highly subjective task, the result has intriguing implications. It provides novel insight into how people interpret and conceptualize discourse about abuse, while it also innovatively links text-based annotation to measurement-based physiological annotator data. From this perspective, the study results suggest that co-collecting measurement-based annotator data with text-based annotations may help support annotations on emotional semantic topics.

6   Conclusion

Social media texts are an information-rich source for research in IPV. We report on a new data collection approach that integrates physiological sensors with human annotation of stakeholders and emotions conveyed in the text vs. felt by the reader. We also integrated human and computer semantic interpretation, and showed how coreference resolution and SRL can be effectively introduced to aid analysis of players in texts narrat-

ing about IPV. The subjects generally agreed on stakeholder labels, and analysis of extracted stakeholder coreference chains provide insights about IPV not readily available from surveys. Stakeholder classification showed modest improvement when using semantic role features over unigrams from coreference chains; future work is needed to improve the classifier using a larger dataset.

Also, GSR differences between trials–with stronger response for IPV texts–provided sensor-based indicators that supported differences found across trials for human emotion annotation and in automated linguistic analysis. Broadly, the results ask the question, left for future work, if measurement-based sensors are a path to counter validity concerns in subjective text annotation tasks.

Acknowledgments

This material is based upon work supported by the National Science Foundation under Award No. IIS-1559889. Any opinions, findings, and conclusions or recommendations expressed in this material are those of the authors and do not necessarily reflect the views of the National Science Foundation.

References

Michele C. Black, Kathleen C. Basile, Matthew J. Breiding, Sharon G. Smith, Mikel L. Walters, Melissa T. Merrick, Jieru Chen, and Mark R. Stevens. 2011. National intimate partner and sexual violence survey. *Centers for Disease Control and Prevention*, 75.

David Finkelhor, Anne Shattuck, Heather A. Turner, and Sherry L. Hamby. 2014. The lifetime prevalence of child sexual abuse and sexual assault assessed in late adolescence. *Journal of Adolescent Health*, 55(3):329–333.

Shannon Greenwood, Andrew Perrin, and Maeve Duggan. 2016. Social media update 2016. Pew Research Center: Internet, Science & Tech.

Etienne G. Krug, Linda L. Dahlberg, James A. Mercy, Anthony B. Zwi, and Rafael Lozano, editors. 2002. *World report on violence and health*. World Health Organization.

Christopher Manning, Mihai Surdeanu, John Bauer, Jenny Finkel, Steven Bethard, and David McClosky. 2014. The Stanford CoreNLP natural language processing toolkit. In *Proceedings of 52nd Annual*

Meeting of the Association for Computational Linguistics: System Demonstrations, pages 55–60, Baltimore, Maryland, June. Association for Computational Linguistics.

Robert Plutchik. 2001. The nature of emotions. *American Scientist*, 89(4):344–350.

Vasin Punyakanok, Dan Roth, and Wen-tau Yih. 2008. The importance of syntactic parsing and inference in semantic role labeling. *Computational Linguistics*, 34(2):257–287.

Johnna Rizza. 2009. Beyond Duluth: A broad spectrum of treatment for a broad spectrum of domestic violence. *Montana Law Review*, 70:125–146.

Nicolas Schrading, Cecilia Ovesdotter Alm, Ray Ptucha, and Christopher Homan. 2015a. An analysis of domestic abuse discourse on Reddit. In *Proceedings of the 2015 Conference on Empirical Methods in Natural Language Processing*, pages 2577–2583, Lisbon, Portugal, September. Association for Computational Linguistics.

Nicolas Schrading, Cecilia Ovesdotter Alm, Raymond Ptucha, and Christopher Homan. 2015b. #WhyIStayed, #WhyILeft: Microblogging to make sense of domestic abuse. In *Proceedings of the 2015 Conference of the North American Chapter of the Association for Computational Linguistics: Human Language Technologies*, pages 1281–1286, Denver, Colorado, May–June. Association for Computational Linguistics.

Yu Shi, Natalie Ruiz, Ronnie Taib, Eric Choi, and Fang Chen. 2007. Galvanic skin response (gsr) as an index of cognitive load. In *CHI '07 Extended Abstracts on Human Factors in Computing Systems*, CHI EA '07, pages 2651–2656, New York, NY, USA. ACM.

Yla R. Tausczik and James W. Pennebaker. 2010. The psychological meaning of words: LIWC and computerized text analysis methods. *Journal of Language and Social Psychology*, 29(1):24–54.

D. H. Taylor. 1964. Drivers' galvanic skin response and the risk of accident. *Ergonomics*, 7(4):439–451.

Intension, Attitude, and Tense Annotation in a High-Fidelity Semantic Representation

Gene Kim and Lenhart Schubert
University of Rochester
Department of Computer Science
{gkim21,schubert}@cs.rochester.edu

Abstract

This paper describes current efforts in developing an annotation schema and guidelines for sentences in Episodic Logic (EL). We focus on important distinctions for representing modality, attitudes, and tense and present an annotation schema that makes these distinctions. EL has proved competitive with other logical formulations in speed and inference-enablement, while expressing a wider array of natural language phenomena including intensional modification of predicates and sentences, propositional attitudes, and tense and aspect.

1 Introduction

Episodic Logic (EL) is a semantic representation and knowledge representation that extends FOL to more closely match the expressivity of natural languages. It echoes both the surface form of language, and more crucially, the semantic types that are found in all languages. Some semantic theorists view the fact that noun phrases denoting both concrete and abstract entities can appear as predicate arguments (*Aristotle, humanity, the fact that there is water on Mars*) as grounds for treating all noun phrases as being of higher types (e.g., second-order predicates). EL instead uses a small number of reification operators to map predicate and sentence intensions to individuals. As a result, quantification remains first-order (but allows quantified phrases such as *most people who smoke*, or *hardly any errors*). Another distinctive feature of EL is that it treats the relation between sentences and episodes (including events, situations, and processes) as a *characterizing relation*, written "**". This coincides with the Davidsonian treatment of events as extra variables of pred-

icates, as long as we restrict ourselves to positive, atomic predications. But it also allows for logically complex characterizations of episodes, such as episodes of not eating anything all day, or of each superpower menacing the other with its nuclear arsenal (Schubert, 2000).

EL has been shown to be suitable for deductive inference, uncertain inference, and Natural-Logic-like inference (Morbini and Schubert, 2009; Schubert and Hwang, 2000; Schubert, 2014). Most recently, Kim and Schubert (2016) developed a system that generated EL verb gloss axioms from WordNet, which enabled inferences that were competitive with the state-of-the-art even with greater expressivity.

In a supplementary document for the above paper, Kim and Schubert present an illustration of EL appropriately handling the intensional predicate modifier *nearly*. The illustration uses the gloss for the second sense of *stumble*, which is *miss a step and fall or nearly fall* and shows that using EL as the representation enables inferences that are not possible using intersective predicate modification.

We are currently underway on an annotation project that is aimed at creating a corpus that can be used to train a reliable, general-purpose ULF (unscoped logical form) transducer. ULF is a preliminary, indexical EL representation with syntactic marking of residual scope ambiguity. If the project is successful, it would overcome the primary limitations of Kim and Schubert's work: scalability and accuracy.

2 Project Overview

Kim and Schubert's system relies in part on manually specified transduction rules that try to construct complete, interpretable sentences from WordNet verb glosses, which are in a stylized,

Proceedings of the Workshop Computational Semantics Beyond Events and Roles (SemBEaR), pages 10–15,
Valencia, Spain, April 4, 2017. ©2017 Association for Computational Linguistics

phrasal form. Often it is not enough to just expand a gloss into a sentence (understandable to a human reader) to enable reliable semantic parsing. The sentence must often be further transformed and broken into multiple, simpler sentences before somewhat reliable semantic parsing is possible. Even then, both the transduction rules and semantic parsing may introduce errors into the resulting definitional axioms(s). Kim and Schubert note that almost a third of the extracted axioms had come from EL formulas that were erroneously transduced from English. These were due to linguistic phenomena that did not show up in the development set or due to sheer sentence complexity. Such errors would become even more of a problem for noun glosses, which can contain quite complex descriptive material. A reliable, general-purpose, semantic parser would eliminate most of this labor and improve the project's scalability. We expect that a statistical semantic parser trained on a large corpus would have better coverage of linguistic phenomena and function robustly for larger sentences.

We plan to annotate several thousand sentences from topically varied sources and have experimented so far with the Brown corpus, the Gigaword newswire corpus and *The Little Prince*. Annotating ULF has many advantages over directly annotating EL logical forms. ULF enables the separation of determining the semantic type structure from replacing indexial expressions and disambiguating quantifier scopes, word senses, and anaphora – tasks which in general require the context of the sentence to resolve. Since we are tackling a range of subtle semantic phenomena beyond those ordinarily considered, this decomposition is likely to achieve better results than a fell-swoop approach. An undisambiguated representation also has the advantage of adaptability to a wide range of tasks – a topic discussed in depth by Bender et al. (2015).

3 Semantic Handling of Intension and Attitudes in EL

This section briefly describes how the semantic interpretation of EL enables proper handling of intension and attitudes. For a fuller description of EL semantics please refer to (Schubert and Hwang, 2000).

3.1 Intensional Modifiers

EL semantic types distinguish *predicate* modifiers from *sentence* modifiers. Predicate modifiers are interpreted as mappings from predicate meanings to predicate meanings, where these are intensional functions based on possible episodes (whose maximal elements are possible worlds). This enables proper interpretation of non-intersective predicate modifiers such as *very*, *fairly*, and *big*, including intensional ones such as *nearly*, *fake*, and *resemble*. For example, EL can express the following fact:

```
(all x [[x (fake.a flower.n)] ⇒
  [(not [x flower.n]) and
   [x (resemble.v flower.n)]]])
```

Similarly, *intensional* sentence modifiers (e.g., *probably*, *according to Fox News*) map sentence intensions to sentence intensions, whereas *extensional* sentence modifiers (e.g., *in the forest*, *at dawn*) become simple predications about episodes upon "deindexing".

3.2 Attitude Predicates

Attitude predicates such as *assert*, *believe*, and *assume* relate an individual to a proposition. Propositions are treated as abstract entities, namely, reified sentence intensions. Of course an attitude predication can be true without the proposition being true. Unlike some semantic representations, EL does not conflate propositions with episodes. Episodes are real (often physical) entities occupying time intervals, whereas propositions are informational entities. Propositions are formed from sentences using a *that* operator, since they are most commonly instantiated as that-clauses in English (e.g., Jim knows *that* there is water on Mars).

4 ULF Syntax

This section will act as a brief introduction to ULF syntax for understanding the examples presented. Atoms in ULF that correspond to lexical entries are followed by a suffix derived from the part of speech. Atoms without the suffix are special EL operators that correspond to particular morpho-syntactic phenomena; see the first visualization in Figure 1 for examples. ULF uses three different brackets: round brackets to indicate prefixed operators, square brackets for sentential formulas with infixed predicates, and angle brackets for (prefixed) operators with ambiguous scope. The sec-

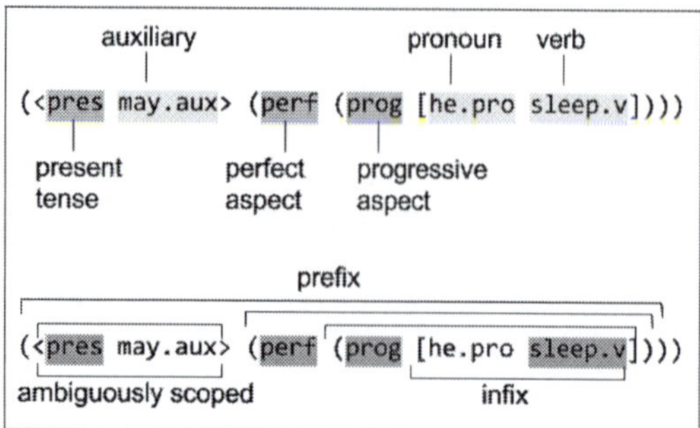

Figure 1: Visualization of ULF syntax for example sentence *He may have been sleeping.* Yellow shows atoms that are represent lexical entries, blue shows special EL operators, and green shows atoms that are acting as the operator in their clauses.

ond visualization in Figure 1 shows a labeling of this. Note that operators can themselves be complex expressions (e.g., `<pres may.aux>`).

5 Annotating Intension and Attitude in ULF

Annotation of modifiers in ULF requires distinguishing predicate modifiers from sentence modifiers, since these have different semantic types. If a modal auxiliary or modal adverb(ial) modifies a sentence without affecting what the sentence predicate says about the subject (e.g., *A major earthquake {may, could} occur; {perhaps, surprisingly, in my opinion} there is no life on Mars*), then it is a sentence-level modifier. If instead the modal auxiliary or adverb(ial) alters the property attributed to the subject, then it must be a predicate-level modifier (e.g., *The cadet must (i.e., is obligated to) obey; the skater {nearly, awkwardly} fell*).

This distinction can be quite subtle since it is dependent on both the lexical entry and the syntax. Consider the following sentences:

(a) "Mary confidently spoke up"

(b) "Mary undoubtedly spoke up"

(c) "Koko is surprisingly intelligent"

(d) "Surprisingly, Koko is intelligent"

In sentence (a) *confidently* is a predicate modifier whereas in sentence (b) *undoubtedly* is a sentence modifier. Clearly, this is entirely determined by the lexical entry since the syntax trees of the

two sentences are identical. Then compare sentence (c) and sentence (d). The only difference between them is the placement of the modifier *surprisingly*, which changes its semantic type.

Annotating attitudes merely requires recognizing when a sentence functions as a propositional argument (rather than, for instance, as an adverbial or relative clause), and using reifying operator *that* accordingly. The operator must be used even if *that* is elided in the surface text: *I'm sure (that) you've heard of him.* Since attitude predicates have the same type structure as extensional predicates, no additional annotation is necessary for ULF. [1]

6 Annotating Aspect and Tense

Aspect is generally captured by the lexical entries in our annotations (e.g., *daily, used to*). However, we introduce *perf* and *prog* as operators for perfect and progressive aspect, since they are generated morpho-syntactically in English, via the auxiliaries *have* and *be* respectively. Semantically, aspect describes the way an event relates to time, so they are sentence modifiers in EL.

EL has two operators for tense – *past* and *pres* – for past and present. We treat the English modal auxiliary *will* as a present-tense verb operating at the sentence level and meaning *at a time after now*.[2] We regard tense as an unscoped operator in ULF (to be "raised" to the sentence level), and consequently it is simply annotated as operating on the verb that bears the tense inflection (this is always the first verb – the head verb – of a tensed verb phrase in English). Some examples:

(a) "He is sleeping"

```
(<pres prog> [he.pro sleep.v])
```

(b) "He has left Rome"

```
(<pres perf> [he.pro (leave.v
Rome.c)])
```

(c) "He had left Rome"

```
(<past perf> [he.pro (leave.v
Rome.c)])
```

(d) "He has been sleeping"

```
(<pres perf> (prog [he.pro
sleep.v]))
```

---

[1] Some clauses used as arguments denote episode types, e.g., *For Mary to be late is unusual*; we distinguish such cases but omit details here.

[2] Formal details of the treatment of tense and temporal adverbials in EL are given in (Hwang and Schubert, 1994).

(e) "He may have been sleeping"

```
(<pres may.aux>
    (perf (prog [he.pro sleep.v]))))
```

Sentence (a) is a simple sentence where the tense is determined by the verb. Sentence (b), (c), and (d) show how *had* and *has* determine the tense of the sentence. Note that in all three cases the perfect auxiliary is followed by the past participle form of the verb. This is simply a syntactic requirement in English. Sentence (e) shows an example where the modal auxiliary determines the tense.

7 Remarks on Strategy

We have experimented with annotating randomly chosen examples from parsed and unparsed corpora such as the Brown corpus, the Gigaword newswire corpus and *The Little Prince*. This experimentation has led to an annotation strategy that starts with phrasal bracketing, followed by adding parts of speech (with manual correction of automatic tagging errors), followed by substituting type-suffixed lexical interpretations for words, followed by addition of any tacit reification and type-shifting operators. Here is a simple example:

```
(Mary (confidently (spoke up)) →
(Mary.nnp (confidently.rb
        (spoke.vbd up.prt))) →
[Mary.prp (confidently.adv-a
        (<past speak_up.v>))].
```

Replacement of *confidently.adv-a* by *undoubtedly.adv-s* would cause subsequent automatic "raising" of the adverb to the sentence level.

Development of annotator tools, such as a possible role supplier for common words and access to the extant semantic parser, as well as evaluation of the described annotation strategy are underway. In parallel, ULF annotation methods of more linguistic phenomena are being developed. For these reasons, the annotation guidelines will not yet be publicly released. Also, since the phenomena described in this document cannot be annotated in isolation in our framework, there are no semantic category-specific preliminary annotations to report.

We expect the annotation effort to be successful because ULF is syntactically close to surface English and the annotator tools under development will simplify the annotation task. Similarly, we expect machine translation methods such as Synchronous Tree Substitution Grammars (Eisner, 2003; Gildea, 2003) to be successful in automating this annotation because of the close syntactic correspondence to the surface form.

8 Generalization to Other Languages

In view of its English-like syntax, our annotation scheme it will not map directly to other languages. For example, Mandarin does not have grammatical tense markers, relying on lexical operators instead. This is in clear contrast with how our annotation schema marks tense on the verb. Of course, languages also differ in their vocabulary and surface operator-operand structure. Thus our corpus will not be cross-lingual.

However, the superficial tense operators of ULF are reduced to more fundamental constructs (predications about episodes) by deindexing, and in general conversion from ULF to ELF yields representations intended to be language-independent in terms of semantic types. The expressive devices employed in those representations, such as event reference, general quantification, reification, and modification are shared by all languages. Generalizing our work to other languages will require developing a ULF for the target language, close to its surface form, and methods of converting the ULF to ELF (in context). This is not a trivial task, but the resulting formulas will be type-coherent and capable of supporting inference.

9 Related Work

Previous efforts have been made toward training a transducer for broad coverage meaning representation of sentences, perhaps most prominently OntoNotes (Hovy et al., 2006) and AMR (Banarescu et al., 2013). These representations employed PropBank, WordNet, VerbNet, and FrameNet as semantic resources, but were not designed to be formally interpretable. Semantic types of nodes are not defined, there is no distiction between extension and intension (or between what is real and what is hypothetical), and thus there is no clear basis for inference. The representations also set aside some important linguistic phenomena, such as tense (hence, how events are temporally linked); and quantifiers are added in modifier-like fashion, much as if they were attributes of entities. DeepBank is a corpus of annotations in English Resource Semantics (ERS), which is a canonicalized and grammar-constrained semantic representation (Flickinger et al., 2012). ERS handles a wide-array of linguistic phenomena, while allowing semantic underspecification by using minimal recursion semantics as its metalanguage representation (Copestake et al., 2005). Although ERS is highly descriptive, it lacks machinery for generating general inferences from fully-resolved formulas.

10 Conclusions and Future Work

We have described how some semantically significant, often neglected phenomena of natural language can be captured in Episodic Logic. We outlined some requirements and methods for annotating a topically broad corpus with unscoped versions of EL, to be used as a basis for training a high-fidelity semantic parser for English. Because EL (and even more so, ULF) is close in form to the surface text, use of machine translation techniques should yield good performance for such a machine learning task. As noted earlier, we believe that a divide-and-conquer approach to resolving various sorts of residual indeterminacy in ULFs is likely to achieve better results than a fell-swoop approach, particularly since we are tackling a range of subtle semantic phenomena beyond those ordinarily considered. High-fidelity interpretations of NL into EL would greatly facilitate many NL applications, including knowledge extraction from lexical and encyclopedic sources, as well as text and dialogue understanding tasks.

11 Acknowledgements

This work was supported by a Sproull Graduate Fellowship from the University of Rochester, DARPA CwC subcontract W911NF-15-1-0542, and NSF EAGER grant IIS-1543758. We are also grateful to the anonymous reviewers for their comments.

References

Laura Banarescu, Claire Bonial, Shu Cai, Madalina Georgescu, Kira Griffitt, Ulf Hermjakob, Kevin Knight, Philipp Koehn, Martha Palmer, and Nathan Schneider. 2013. Abstract Meaning Representation for sembanking. In *Proceedings of the 7th Linguistic Annotation Workshop and Interoperability with Discourse*, pages 178–186, Sofia, Bulgaria, August. Association for Computational Linguistics.

Emily M. Bender, Dan Flickinger, Stephan Oepen, Woodley Packard, and Ann Copestake. 2015. Layers of interpretation: On grammar and compositionality. In *Proceedings of the 11th International Conference on Computational Semantics*, pages 239–249, London, UK, April. Association for Computational Linguistics.

Ann Copestake, Dan Flickinger, Carl Pollard, and Ivan A. Sag. 2005. Minimal Recursion Semantics: An introduction. *Research on Language and Computation*, 3(2):281–332.

Jason Eisner. 2003. Learning non-isomorphic tree mappings for machine translation. In *The Companion Volume to the Proceedings of 41st Annual Meeting of the Association for Computational Linguistics*, pages 205–208, Sapporo, Japan, July. Association for Computational Linguistics.

Dan Flickinger, Yi Zhang, and Valia Kordoni. 2012. Deepbank. a dynamically annotated treebank of the Wall Street Journal. In *Proceedings of the 11th International Workshop on Treebanks and Linguistic Theories*, pages 85–96.

Daniel Gildea. 2003. Loosely tree-based alignment for machine translation. In *Proceedings of the 41st Annual Meeting of the Association for Computational Linguistics*, pages 80–87, Sapporo, Japan, July. Association for Computational Linguistics.

Eduard Hovy, Mitchell Marcus, Martha Palmer, Lance Ramshaw, and Ralph Weischedel. 2006. Ontonotes: The 90% solution. In *Proceedings of the Human Language Technology Conference of the NAACL, Companion Volume: Short Papers*, pages 57–60, New York City, USA, June. Association for Computational Linguistics.

Chung Hee Hwang and Lenhart K. Schubert. 1994. Interpreting tense, aspect and time adverbials: A compositional, unified approach. In *Proceedings of the First International Conference on Temporal Logic*, ICTL '94, pages 238–264, London, UK, UK. Springer-Verlag.

Gene Kim and Lenhart Schubert. 2016. High-fidelity lexical axiom construction from verb glosses. In *Proceedings of the Fifth Joint Conference on Lexical and Computational Semantics*, pages 34–44, Berlin, Germany, August. Association for Computational Linguistics.

Fabrizio Morbini and Lenhart Schubert. 2009. Evaluation of Epilog: A reasoner for Episodic Logic. In *Proceedings of the Ninth International Symposium on Logical Formalizations of Commonsense Reasoning*, Toronto, Canada, June.

Lenhart K. Schubert and Chung Hee Hwang. 2000. Episodic logic meets little red riding hood: A comprehensive natural representation for language understanding. In Lucja M. Iwańska and Stuart C. Shapiro, editors, *Natural Language Processing and*

Knowledge Representation, pages 111–174. MIT
Press, Cambridge, MA, USA.

Lenhart K. Schubert. 2000. The situations we talk
about. In Jack Minker, editor, *Logic-based Artifi-
cial Intelligence*, pages 407–439. Kluwer Academic
Publishers, Norwell, MA, USA.

Lenhart Schubert. 2014. From treebank parses to
Episodic Logic and commonsense inference. In
*Proceedings of the ACL 2014 Workshop on Semantic
Parsing*, pages 55–60, Baltimore, MD, June. Asso-
ciation for Computational Linguistics.

Towards a lexicon of event-selecting predicates for a French FactBank

Ingrid Falk and Fabienne Martin
University of Stuttgart
`firstname.lastname@ling.uni-stuttgart.de`

Abstract

This paper presents ongoing work for the construction of a French FactBank and a lexicon of French event-selecting predicates (ESPs), by applying the factuality detection algorithm introduced in (Saurí and Pustejovsky, 2012). This algorithm relies on a lexicon of ESPs, specifying how these predicates influence the factuality of their embedded events. For this pilot study, we focused on French factive and implicative verbs, and capitalised on a lexical resource for the English counterparts of these verbs provided by the CSLI Group (Nairn et al., 2006; Karttunen, 2012).

1 Introduction

Texts not only describe events, but also encode information conveying whether the events described correspond to real situations in the world, or to uncertain, (im)probable or (im)possible situations. This level of information concerns *event factuality*. This study reports ongoing work on the annotation of French TimeBank events with event factuality information, whose main goal is the elaboration of a French FactBank. We plan to achieve this as follows. Saurí and Pustejovsky (2012) developed an elaborate model of event factuality that allows for its automatic detection. We aim to capitalise on this work by applying Saurí and Pustejovsky (2012)'s algorithm to the events in the French TimeBank (FTiB henceforth) and assign to these a factuality profile. Given that the FTiB has only about 1/4 of the size of the English Time-Bank, we will manually review the automatically obtained factuality profiles in a second step.

Saurí and Pustejovsky (2012)'s algorithm relies on two crucial prerequisites. The first is the identification of the *sources* at play, i.e. the cognitive agents endorsing a specific epistemic stance on the events described. The text author is the default source, but some linguistic constructions — and a subclass of verbs in particular, see e.g. *affirm* — present one or more sources that are also committed to the factuality of the reported event. Secondly, the algorithm makes use of three language-specific and manually developed *lexical resources*, capturing the way polarity particles, particles of epistemic modality and so-called event-selecting predicates (e.g. *manage to, suspect that*) influence event factuality. In this study, we show how existing lexical semantic resources can be used and modified in order to build the French-specific lexical resources needed to apply Saurí and Pustejovski's algorithm to the French TimeBank.

2 The English FactBank

As described in (Saurí and Pustejovsky, 2009), FactBank is an English corpus annotated with information concerning the factuality of events. It is built on top of the English TimeBank by adding a level of semantic information. TimeBank is a corpus annotated with TimeML (Pustejovsky et al., 2005), a specification language representing temporal and event information in discourse. The factuality information encoded in TimeBank and relevant for our work are the event-selecting predicates (cf. Section 3) which project a factual value to the embedded event by means of subordination links (or SLINKs).

In TimeBank, a total of 9 488 events across 208 newspaper texts have been manually identified and annotated. FactBank assigns additional factuality information to these events. More specifically, it is annotated for each event (i) whether its factuality is assessed by a source different from the text author and (ii) the degree of factuality the new source and the text author attribute to the event (for in-

Proceedings of the Workshop Computational Semantics Beyond Events and Roles (SemBEaR), pages 16–21,
Valencia, Spain, April 4, 2017. ©2017 Association for Computational Linguistics

stance, *Peter affirmed P* presents *P* as certain for Peter, but does not commit the text author to *P* in a specific way). Saurí and Pustejovsky (2009) distinguish six 'committed' factuality values (i.e. values to which a source is committed) and one 'uncommitted' value, which are shown in Table 1.

Saurí and Pustejovsky (2012) present an algorithm which assigns to each TimeBank event a factuality profile consisting of (i) its factuality value, (ii) the source(s) assigning the factuality value to that event and (iii) the time at which the factuality value assignment takes place. The algorithm assumes that events and relevant sources are already identified and computes the factuality profile of events by modelling the effect of factuality relations across levels of syntactic embedding. It crucially relies on three lexical resources which the authors developed manually for English. Since to apply this algorithm to the French data we need to create similar resources for French, we describe them in more detail in the following section.

3 Lexical Resources for the Automatic Detection of Factuality Profiles

The first lexical resource is a list of 11 negation particles (adverbs, determiners and pronouns) which determine the polarity of the context, together with a language independent table showing how these polarity markers influence the polarity of the event. The corresponding list of negation particles needed for French can be set up easily.

The second resource aims to capture the influence of epistemic *modality* on the event. It gives a list of 31 adjectives, adverbs and verbs of epistemic modality together with the factuality value they express. Most of their French counterparts influence the context the same way as in English, except for modal verbs, that are well-known to give rise to an 'actuality entailment' under their root/non-epistemic readings (i.e. to present the embedded event as a fact in the real world) when combined with a perfective tense, see (Hacquard, 2009), an issue briefly addressed in Section 4.

The third resource is the most complex one and accounts for the influence on the event factuality value in cases where the event is embedded by so-called *event-selecting predicates (ESPs)*, of which *suspect that/manage to* are examples. ESPs are predicates with an event-denoting argument, which lexically specify the factuality of the event. Saurí and Pustejovsky distinguish two kinds of

ESPs: *Source Introducing Predicates (SIPs)* introduce a new source in discourse (e.g. *suspect/believe*); *Non Source Introducing Predicates (NSIPs)* do not (e.g. *manage/fail*). As part of their lexical semantics, SIPs determine (i) the factuality value the new source (the 'cogniser') assigns to the event described by the complement, and (ii) the factuality value assigned by the text author (i.e. the 'anchor') to the same event. NSIPs, on the other hand, determine event factuality wrt. a unique source, the anchor. In addition, the assessment of event factuality wrt. the relevant source(s) varies with the polarity and modality present in the context of the ESP. Table 1 illustrates the lexicon layout through sample entries for the NSIPs *manage* and *fail*.[1] The ESP lexicon built by Saurí and Pustejovsky (2012) consists of 646 entries in total (393 verbs, 165 nouns and 88 adjectives). In order to apply Saurí and Pustejovsky (2012)'s algorithm to the French TimeBank, we need to build a similar ESP lexicon for French. To speed up this process, we plan to use a large body of research about English predicates with sentential complements (Karttunen, 1971b; Karttunen, 1971a; Nairn et al., 2006; Karttunen, 2012)[2], which we briefly introduce in the following.

Factive and implicative verbs. Nairn et al. (2006) develop a semantic classification of complement-taking verbs according to their effect on the polarity of their complement clauses. This classification is shown in Table 2. We illustrate how the table works in the following examples. In example (1), the ESP *fail to* has positive polarity. We obtain the factuality of the embedded event (*reschedule*) by retrieving from the polarity + column in Table 2 the polarity value in the *fail to* row, which is '−', i.e. the meeting is not rescheduled (has factuality CT−). For (2), the factuality must be retrieved from the polarity − column resulting in '+', i.e. a factuality of CT+ (the meeting is rescheduled).

(1) Kim *failed to* <u>reschedule</u> the meeting.

(2) Kim did not *fail to* <u>reschedule</u> the meeting.

The effect of a predicate on the polarity of its embedded complement is represented more concisely

---

[1] The lexicon layout for SIPs, less relevant for our study, is very similar except that an SIP lexicon entry must also provide factuality values for the cogniser source in addition to the anchor.

[2] The ESP lexicons created in (Saurí and Pustejovsky, 2012) are not freely available.

Contextual factuality											
	CT			PR			PS			U		
polarity	+	−	u	+	−	u	+	−	u	+	−	u
manage (a)	CT+	CT−	CTu	PR+	PR−	PRu	PS+	PS−	PSu	Uu	Uu	Uu
fail (a)	CT−	CT+	CTu	PR−	PR+	PRu	PS−	PS+	PSu	Uu	Uu	Uu

Table 1: Sample lexical entries for NSIPs. CT, PR and PS signify certain, probable and possible respectively, U (and/or u) unspecified (unknown or uncommitted), (a) refers to the anchor.

	Polarity of ESP		Sample
	+	−	predicate
2-way	+	−	*manage to*
implicatives	−	+	*fail to*
1-way	+	n	*force to*
+implicatives	−	n	*refuse to*
1-way	n	−	*attempt to*
-implicatives	n	+	*hesitate to*
factives	+	+	*forget that*
counterfactives	−	−	*pretend that*
Neutral	n	n	*want to*

Table 2: Semantic classification of complement taking verbs wrt. the effect of the polarity of the main clause (ESP, head row) on the factuality of the complement clause (embedded event, subsequent rows). n stands for none.

through a "signature". For instance, the signature of factive verbs as *forget that* is '$++|-+$' (Read: 'if positive polarity, event happens; if negative polarity, event happens').

Thus, based on the signature of a predicate and its polarity in a given sentence, we can determine the factuality of the embedded event in that sentence. It should now be obvious how the classification in Table 2 can be "plugged" into the ESP lexical resources illustrated in Table 1:[3] For a given ESP for which a lexical entry has to be set up (*eg. fail*), the factuality value conveyed on the embedded event can be retrieved from Table 2 whenever the corresponding table entry is not n. In case it is, the polarity value must be set to u (unspecified).

Nairn et al. (2006) compiled a list of roughly 250 English verbs found to carry some kind of implication: a positive or negative entailment, a factive or a counterfactive presupposition[4]. To test how this approach can help us build the French ESP lexical resource required for a French factuality profiler, we translated these English verbs into

their French counterparts, and looked at the sentences in the French TimeBank using these French counterparts as ESPs. We first briefly introduce the French TimeBank before describing our data, experiments and findings.

4 Experiments on the French TimeBank

The French TimeBank (Bittar, 2010; Bittar et al., 2011) is built on the same principles as the English TimeBank, but introduces additional markup language to deal with linguistic phenomena not yet covered and specific to French. Most relevant to this study are the following. FTiB uses ALINK elements to encode aspectual subordination relations, holding between events realised by an aspectual verb (e.g. *commencer* 'begin') and a subordinated event complement. The subordinating events in ALINKs, as those in SLINKs, are ESPs and are therefore also relevant for this study. Also, since French modal auxiliaries can be fully inflected and fall within the scope of aspectual operators, they are also marked up as events. Lastly, the TimeML schema was adapted to represent the grammatical tense/aspect system of French, and to account *eg.* for the *imparfait* (IMPERFECT), not grammaticalised in English.

FTiB is made up of 108 newspaper texts for a total of 16 208 tokens. 2 098 of these represent events. Since in our experiments, we are interested in assessing factuality at the sentence level, we segmented FTiB into (814) sentences, and extracted from them the subordination links (SLINKs and ALINKs). Overall, FTiB contains 485 subordination links. Luckily, the subordinating events in 444 of these links are ESPs. From these links, we selected those where the subordinating event was a translation of an English verb for which we have a signature (179, instantiating 49 different verbs). We first checked for the 49 types whether the French predicate has the same signature as the English verb it translates. We found that this was very roughly the case for most of

---

[3]Factive and implicative verbs are typically non-source introducing predicates (NSIPs).

[4]These resources are available at https://web.stanford.edu/group/csli_lnr/Lexical_Resources/.

these verbs (but see below). For example, the factive signature '$++ \mid -+$' of *learn that* is inherited by its translation *apprendre que*. Similarly, the implicative signature '$+- \mid -$n' of *help* also characterises its French translation *aider à*. Our translation approach raised several interesting issues, however. A first one concerns verbs with a syntax-dependent factuality profile. In English, *learn that/forget that* for instance have the (factive) signature $++ \mid -+$, whereas *learn to* is less biased wrt. the factuality of the embedded event, and *forget to* has the (implicative) signature $+- \mid -+$. French translations of these verbs also quite systematically see their signatures varying with the syntactic structure, or have an argument structure that its English counterpart cannot instantiate; see e.g. the factive VP *apprendre sa mort* (lit. '*learn his death*'). For these cases, we paired the relevant reading with the appropriate signature manually. A second issue is raised by verbs with an aspect-dependent factuality profile. It is well-known that in Romance, modal verbs trigger an actuality entailment under some of their readings, but *with a perfective only*. For instance, the example (3), where the modal verb *permettre* has an *enable* reading and is combined with a perfective (PFV), triggers an actuality entailment (the embedded event has to happen). With an imperfective (IMP), however, the actuality entailment vanishes, cf. (4). Also, when the same verb *permettre* has a deontic ('grant permission') reading, no actuality entailment is triggered, even with a perfective, see (5) (Hacquard 2006:41).

(3) *Cette   carte   **m'a permis**   d'entrer.*
This   card   me permit-PFV   to enter
→ I entered.

(4) *Cette   carte   **me permettait**   d'entrer.*
This   card   me permit-IMP   to enter
↛ I entered.

(5) *Le   doyen   **m'a permis**   d'entrer.*
The   dean   me permit-PFV   to enter
↛ I entered.

Our translations of the English verbs analysed by Nairn et al. (2006) revealed that several other French verbs show the same lability, see Table 3. That is, the entailment triggered with the perfective is lost with an imperfective, or at least replaced by a defeasible inference, see e.g. the examples (6)-(7).

	ASPECT USED			
	PFV		IMP	
	Polarity of ESP			
	+	−	+	−
assurer (la victoire) insure (the victory)	+	n	n	n
condamner (x à rester) condemn (*x* to stay)	+	n	n	n
conduire (à la catastrophe) lead to (catastrophy)	+	n	n	n
apprendre (à voler) learn (to fly)	+*	−*	n	n
réussir (à entrer) manage (to enter)	+	−	n	n
daigner (répondre) deign (to answer)	+	−	n	n
motiver (x à venir) motivate (*x* to come)	+*	−*	n	n
échouer (à persuader x) fail (to persuade *x*)	−	+	n	n

Table 3: Examples of verbs whose inferential profile varies with the aspect used. Certain events are labelled '+', very likely but not certain events, '+*', counterfactual events, −, very unlikely events '−*'.

(6) *A   ce   moment-là,   elle **a réussi**   à*
at   that   moment   she   manage-**PFV**   to
s'enfuir. #Mais finalement, elle
escape   but   finally   she
ne s'est pas enfuie.
NEG escape-PFV
'At that moment, she managed to escape.
But finally, she didn't escape.'

(7) *A   ce   moment-là,   elle **réussissait***
at   that   moment   she   manage-**IMP**
(encore) à   s'enfuir. OK Mais
(still)   to   escape   but
finalement, elle ne s'est pas enfuie.
finally   she   NEG escape-PFV
'At that moment, she 'was managing' to
escape. But finally, she didn't escape.'

Interestingly, most of these predicates with an aspect-dependent inferential profile (12 out of 13 in the current stage of annotation) are implicative verbs. On the other hand, verbs whose inferential profile is independent from aspect are mostly factive ($++ \mid -+$) verbs (17 out of 23). The verb *savoir* illustrates well the point. Used as a translation of the English factive verb *know*, *savoir* is factive both with PFV and IMP. However, *savoir* is also used in the FTiB as a two-way implicative verb ($++ \mid --$), see (8)-(9). In the latter use, *savoir* has an abilitative reading and like *être capable de* 'be able to', triggers an actuality entailment with PFV, see (8), but has a neutral inferential profile with IMP $(+n| - n)$, see (9).

(8) *Il a su   maîtriser ce   fantasme.*
     he   be able-**PFV** master   this fantasy
     → He mastered this fantasy.

(9) *Il savait   maîtriser ce   fantasme.*
     he   be able-**IMP** master   this fantasy
     ↛ He mastered this fantasy.

Why do implicative verbs (contrary to factive verbs) lose their entailment when combined with IMP? Recent analyses of implicative verbs by (Baglini and Francez, 2016) and (Nadathur, 2016) can help to explain this observation. According to Baglini & Francez' analysis, a *manage p* statement *presupposes* familiarity with a causally necessary but insufficient condition *A* for the truth of *p*, and *asserts* that *A* actually caused the truth of *p*. Nadathur extends a modified version of this analysis to the whole class of implicative verbs. The important point for us is that under these analyses, implicative verbs have an at-issue component: they assert an 'event', namely the obtaining/actualisation of the causal factor *A* for the truth of *p*. Given the 'imperfective paradox', the imperfective form of such verbs unsurprisingly *suspends* the actualisation event, as what happens with the imperfective form of overtly causative verbs (e.g. *Trump was causing a new catastrophe when Pence stopped him* does not entail the occurrence of a new catastrophe). On the other hand, factive verbs like *savoir que p* 'know that *p*' do not assert the obtaining of a causal factor for the truth of *p*, but rather a mental state having *p* as its object. We therefore do not expect aspect to interfere with their inferential profile.

For these verbs with an aspect-dependent aspectual profile (including plainly modal ones)[5], we manually annotated the reading instantiated and the corresponding signature in the FTiB.

The third interesting point raised by our translation is illustrated by French verbs having a different factuality profile than their English counterparts. For instance, although *pousser à* is used to translate the implicative verb *provoke to*, it is not implicative with an agent subject, even with a perfective (contrary to its near synonym *conduire à*).

---

[5]FTiB has only 32 instances of *devoir*, 8 of *falloir* and 21 of *pouvoir*.

5 Ongoing research

These experiments showed that verbs whose factuality profile varies with the reading selected and/or its argument structure are very pervasive among French ESPs. A lexicon of ESPs should therefore carefully distinguish between the different readings/argument structures an ESP may instantiate. Also, they suggest that interesting new correlations can be found between event factuality profiles on one hand, and particular sets of syntactic/semantic properties on the other. For instance, verbs like *refuser* 'refuse/fail' are two way implicative verbs with an inanimate subject or with an animate subject controlling the complement, cf. (10)-(11), but only trigger a strong (but nevertheless defeasible) inference with a matrix subject distinct from the infinitival subject, see (12).

(10) *Le tiroir **a refusé** de s'ouvrir, #mais il s'est
      ouvert quand même.*
      'The drawer failed to open, but it opened
      nevertheless.'

(11) *Marie **a refusé** d'entrer, #mais elle est
      entrée quand même.*
      'Marie refused to enter, but she entered
      nevertheless.'

(12) *Le garde **a refusé que** Marie entre, OK mais
      elle est entrée quand même.*
      'The guard refused to allow Marie to enter,
      but she entered nevertheless.'

To find these correlations, we are building a French lexicon of ESPs on top of a rich lexicon encoding morphological, syntactic and semantic properties of French verbs *for each of their readings*, "Les verbes français" (Dubois and Dubois-Charlier, 1997; François et al., 2007). In the first step, we use the French verbs analysed in our experiments as seeds, link them with each of their readings in *Les verbes français*, and provide a manual signature for all of their other ESP readings. This will hopefully give an idea of the semantic and syntactic properties characterising each factuality profile. In the second step, we will enrich the different subclasses of ESPs (distinguished by their signature) with similar candidates by using (semi-)automatic methods along the lines of those described in (Richardson and Kuhn, 2012; De Melo and De Paiva, 2014; White and Rawlins, 2016; Eckle-Kohler, 2016), and then review them manually.

References

Rebekah Baglini and Itamar Francez. 2016. The Implications of Managing. *Journal of Semantics*, 33/3:541–560.

André Bittar, Pascal Amsili, Pascal Denis, and Laurence Danlos. 2011. French TimeBank: an ISO-TimeML annotated reference corpus. In *Proceedings of the 49th Annual Meeting of the Association for Computational Linguistics: Human Language Technologies: short papers-Volume 2*, pages 130–134. Association for Computational Linguistics.

André Bittar. 2010. *Building a TimeBank for French: a reference corpus annotated according to the ISO-TimeML standard*. Ph.D. thesis, Paris 7.

Gerard De Melo and Valeria De Paiva. 2014. Sense-specific implicative commitments. In *International Conference on Intelligent Text Processing and Computational Linguistics*, pages 391–402. Springer.

Jean Dubois and Françoise Dubois-Charlier. 1997. *Les Verbes français*. Larousse.

Judith Eckle-Kohler. 2016. Verbs Taking Clausal and Non-Finite Arguments as Signals of Modality - Revisiting the Issue of Meaning Grounded in Syntax. In *Proceedings of the 54th Annual Meeting of the Association for Computational Linguistics, ACL 2016, August 7-12, 2016, Berlin, Germany, Volume 1: Long Papers*.

Jacques François, Denis Le Pesant, and Danielle Leeman. 2007. Présentation de la classification des Verbes Français de Jean Dubois et Françoise Dubois-Charlier. *Langue française*, 153(1):3–19.

Valentine Hacquard. 2009. On the Interaction of Aspect and Modal Auxiliaries. *Linguistics and Philosophy*, 32:279–312.

Lauri Karttunen. 1971a. Implicative Verbs. *Language*, 47(2):340–358.

Lauri Karttunen. 1971b. *The logic of English predicate complement constructions*, volume 4. Indiana University Linguistics Club Bloomington, Indiana.

Lauri Karttunen. 2012. Simple and phrasal implicatives. In *Proceedings of the First Joint Conference on Lexical and Computational Semantics-Volume 1: Proceedings of the main conference and the shared task, and Volume 2: Proceedings of the Sixth International Workshop on Semantic Evaluation*, pages 124–131. Association for Computational Linguistics.

Prerna Nadathur. 2016. Causal necessity and sufficiency in implicativity. In *Proceedings of Semantics and Linguistics Theory (SALT) 26*, pages 1002–1021.

Rowan Nairn, Cleo Condoravdi, and Lauri Karttunen. 2006. Computing relative polarity for textual inference. In *Proceedings of the Fifth International workshop on Inference in Computational Semantics (ICoS-5)*, pages 20–21.

James Pustejovsky, Robert Knippen, Jessica Littman, and Roser Saurí. 2005. Temporal and event information in natural language text. *Language resources and evaluation*, 39(2):123–164.

Kyle Richardson and Jonas Kuhn. 2012. Light textual inference for semantic parsing. In *24th International Conference on Computational Linguistics*, page 1007.

Roser Saurí and James Pustejovsky. 2009. FactBank: a corpus annotated with event factuality. *Language resources and evaluation*, 43(3):227.

Roser Saurí and James Pustejovsky. 2012. Are you sure that this happened? assessing the factuality degree of events in text. *Computational Linguistics*, 38(2):261–299.

Aaron Steven White and Kyle Rawlins. 2016. A computational model of s-selection. In *Semantics and Linguistic Theory*, volume 26, pages 641–663.

Universal Dependencies to Logical Forms with Negation Scope

Federico Fancellu   **Siva Reddy**   **Adam Lopez**   **Bonnie Webber**
ILCC, School of Informatics, University of Edinburgh
f.fancellu@sms.ed.ac.uk, siva.reddy@ed.ac.uk, {alopez, bonnie}@inf.ed.ac.uk

Abstract

Many language technology applications would benefit from the ability to represent negation and its scope on top of widely-used linguistic resources. In this paper, we investigate the possibility of obtaining a first-order logic representation with negation scope marked using *Universal Dependencies*. To do so, we enhance *UDepLambda*, a framework that converts dependency graphs to logical forms. The resulting *UDepLambda¬* is able to handle phenomena related to scope by means of an higher-order type theory, relevant not only to negation but also to universal quantification and other complex semantic phenomena. The initial conversion we did for English is promising, in that one can represent the scope of negation also in the presence of more complex phenomena such as universal quantifiers.

1 Introduction

Amongst the different challenges around the topic of negation, detecting and representing its scope is one that has been extensively researched in different sub-fields of NLP (e.g. Information Extraction (Velldal et al., 2012; Fancellu et al., 2016)). In particular, recent work have acknowledged the value of representing the scope of negation on top of existing linguistic resources (e.g. AMR – Bos (2016)). Manually annotating the scope of negation is however a time-consuming process, requiring annotators to have some expertise of formal semantics.

Our solution to this problem is to automatically convert an available representation that captures negation into a framework that allows a rich variety of semantic phenomena to be represented, in-

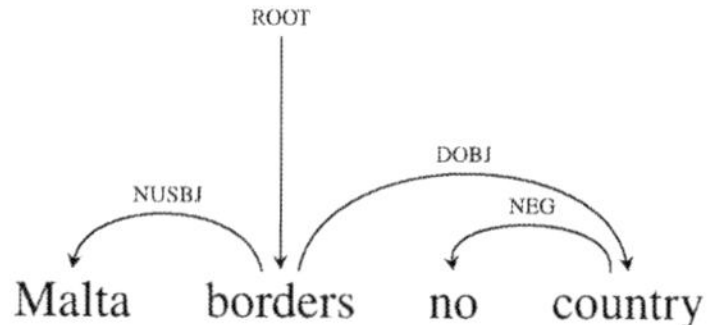

(a) UD Dependency Tree

$$\lambda e.\exists x \exists y.borders(e) \wedge country(x) \wedge no(x) \wedge$$
$$Malta(y) \wedge arg1(e,y) \wedge arg2(e,x)$$

(b) UDepLambda Logical Form

$$\forall x.country(x) \rightarrow \neg \exists e \exists y.borders(e) \wedge$$
$$Malta(y) \wedge arg1(e,y) \wedge arg2(e,x)$$

(c) Desired Logical Form

Figure 1: The dependency tree for '*Malta borders no country*' and its logical forms

cluding scope. That is, given an input sentence, we show how its *universal dependency* (UD) parse can be converted into a representation in first-order logic (FOL) with lambda terms that captures both predicate–argument relations and scope.

Our approach is based on *UDepLambda* (Reddy et al., 2017; Reddy et al., 2016), a constraint framework that converts dependency graphs into logical forms, by reducing the lambda expressions assigned to the dependency edges using the lambda expressions of the connected head and child nodes. The edge labels in the input UD graph are only edited minimally so to yield a more fine-grained description on the phenomena they describe, while lexical information is used only for a very restricted class of lexical items, such as negation cues. A FOL representation of the entire input graph can be then obtained by traversing the edges in a given order and combining their semantics.

However, in its original formulation, UDe-

Proceedings of the Workshop Computational Semantics Beyond Events and Roles (SemBEaR), pages 22–32,
Valencia, Spain, April 4, 2017. ©2017 Association for Computational Linguistics

pLambda does not handle either universal quantifiers or other scope phenomena. For example, the sentence 'Malta borders no country' has the UD graph shown in Figure 1(a). When compared to the correct representation given in Figure 1(c), the UDepLambda output shown in Figure 1(b) shows the absence of universal quantification, which in turn leads negation scope to be misrepresented.

For this reason, we set the foundation of **UDepLambda¬** (UDepLambda-*not*), an enhanced version of the original framework, whose type theory allows us to jointly handle negation and universal quantification. Moreover, unlike its predecessor, the logical forms are based on the one used in the 'Groeningen Meaning Bank' (GMB; (Basile et al., 2012a)), so to allow future comparison to a manually annotated semantic bank.

Although the present work shows the conversion process for English, given that the edge labels are *universal*, our framework could be used to explore the problem of representing the scope of negation in the other 40+ languages universal dependencies are available in. This could also address the problem that all existing resources to represent negation scope as a logical form are limited to English (e.g. GMB and 'DeepBank' (Flickinger et al., 2012)) or only to a few other languages (e.g. 'The Spanish Resource Grammar' (Marimon, 2010)).

In the reminder of this paper, after introducing the formalism we will be working in (§3), we will work the theory behind some of the conversion rules, from basic verbal negation to some of the more complex phenomena related to negation scope, such as the determiner 'no' (§4.1), the interaction between the negation operator and the universal classifier (§4.2) and non-adverbial or lexicalized negation cues such as 'nobody', 'nothing' and 'nowhere' (§4.3). Limitations, where present, will be highlighted.

Contribution. The main contribution of the paper is *UDepLambda¬*, a UD-to-FOL conversion framework, whose type theory is able to handle scope related phenomena, which we show here in the case of negation.

Future work. *UDepLambda¬* can serve as a basis for further extensions that could apply to other complex semantic phenomena and be learned automatically, given the link to a manually annotated semantic bank.

2 Related work

Available resources that contain a representation of negation scope can be divided in two types: 1) those that represent negation as a FOL (or FOL-translatable) representation (e.g. GMB, 'DeepBank'), where systems built using these resources are concerned with correctly *representing* FOL variables and predicates in the scope of negation; and 2) those that try to ground negation at a string-level, where both the negation operator and scope are defined as spans of text (Vincze et al., 2008; Morante and Daelemans, 2012). Systems trained on these resources are then concerned with *detecting* these spans of text.

Resources in 1) are limited in that they are only available in English or for a small number of languages. Moreover no attempt has been made to connect them to more widely-used, cross-linguistic frameworks.

On the other hand, grounding a semantic phenomenon to a string-level leads to inevitable simplification. For instance, the interaction between the negation operator and the universal quantifier (e.g. 'Not every staff member is British' vs. 'None of the staff members are British'), along a formal representation that would allow for inference operations is lost. Furthermore, each corpus is tailored to different applications, making annotation styles across corpora incompatible. Nonetheless these resources have been widely used in the field of Information Extraction and in particular in the Bio-Medical domain.

Finally, it is also worth mentioning that there has been some attempts to use formal semantic representations to detect scope at a string level. Packard et al. (2014) used hand-crafted heuristics to traverse the MRS (Minimal Recursion Semantics) structures of negative sentences to then detect which words were in the scope of negation and which were not. Basile et al. (2012b) tried instead to first transform a DRS (Discourse Representation Structure) into graph form and then align this to strings. Whilst the MRS-based system outperformed previous work, mainly due to the fact that MRS structures are closely related to the surface realization, the DRT-based approach performed worse than most systems, mostly given to the fact that the formalism is not easily translatable into a theory-neutral surface-oriented representation.

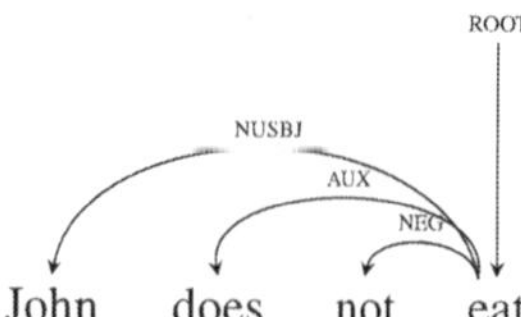

Figure 2: Dependency graph for the sentence 'John does not eat'

3 UDepLambda¬

We introduce here the foundations of *UDepLambda¬*, an enhancement to the *UDepLambda* framework to convert a UD graph into its correspondent logical form. As its predecessor, the conversion takes place in four different steps: *enhancement, binarization, substitution* and *composition*. Whereas binarization and composition are the same as *UDepLambda*, substitution differs in:

- using a higher order type-theory to deal with universal quantification, which can interact with other scope operator such as negation;

- using FOL expressions based on those used in the Groeningen Meaning Bank (GMB), so as to link to a manually–annotated semantic bank which can be leveraged for future work.[1]

The details of the four steps are as follows:

Enhancement. In this step, we first convert a dependency tree to a dependency graph using existing enhancements in UDepLambda. The enhanced dependency labels are represented in red color. In future, we will replace this step with existing enhancements (Schuster and Manning, 2016).

Binarization. The dependency graph is mapped to a LISP-style s-expression, where the order of the edge traversal is specified. For instance, the expression (*nsubj* (*aux* (*neg* eat not) does) John) indicates that the semantic representation of the sentence in Figure (2) is derived by composing the semantics of the edge *nsubj* with the logic form of 'John' and of the phrase 'does

---

not eat'. The semantics of the phrase 'does not eat' is in turn derived by composing the edge *aux* with the phrase 'not eat' and the auxiliary 'does'. Finally 'not' and 'eat' are composed along the edge *neg*.

The order of traversal follows an *obliqueness hierarchy* which defines a strict ordering of the modifiers of a given head traversed during composition. This hierarchy is reminiscent of bottom-up traversal in a binarized constituency tree (where for instance the direct object is always visited before the subject). Furthermore, for a head to be further composed, all its modifiers needs to be composed first. In the sentence in Figure (2), this hierarchy is defined as *neg > aux > nusbj*, where the semantics of the subject can be applied only when the other modifiers to the verb-head have been already composed.

Substitution. The substitution step assigns a lambda expression to each edge and vertex (i.e. word) in the graph. *The lambda expressions of the edges are manually crafted to match the semantics of the edge labels while no assumption is made on the semantics of the word-vertices which are always introduced as existentially bound variables*. This allows us not to rely for most part on any language-specific lexical information. These expressions follows recent work on semantic compositionality of complex phenomena in event semantics (Champollion, 2011). In doing this, we generalize our type theory as follows:

- Each word-vertex is assigned a semantic type $\langle\langle v, t\rangle, t\rangle$ or $\langle\langle v, t\rangle, t\rangle$ (here shortened in $\langle vt, t\rangle$), where v stands for either a paired variable of type Event × Individual. This is in contrast with the type assigned to words in the original UDepLambda $\langle v, t\rangle$. The result of this type-raising operation is clear when we compare the following lambda expressions:

UDepLambda: $\lambda x.man(x_a)$
UDepLambda¬: $\lambda f.\exists x.man(x_a) \wedge f(x)$

where the 'handle' f allows for complex types to be added inside another lambda expression.

Following the GMB, proper nouns are treated like indefinite nouns, being linked to a existentially-bound variable (e.g. John := $\lambda f.\exists x.named(x_a, John, PER) \wedge f(x)$).

- Each edge is assigned the semantic type $\langle\langle vt, t\rangle, \langle\langle vt, t\rangle, \langle vt, t\rangle\rangle\rangle$ where we combine a generalized quantifier over the parent word (P) with the one over the child word (Q) to return another generalized quantifier (f). For instance, when reducing the sub-expression ($nsubj$ eat John), we first reduce the parent vertex 'eat' (P) and then the child vertex 'John'(Q) using the semantics of the subject ('Actor' in the GMB).

  $$nsubj := \lambda P.\lambda Q.\lambda f.P(\lambda x.f(x) \wedge Q(\lambda y.\ Actor(x_e, y_a)))$$

  When compared to the original UDepLambda expression (of type $\langle\langle v, t\rangle, \langle\langle v, t\rangle, \langle v, t\rangle\rangle\rangle$):

  $$\lambda f.\lambda g.\lambda x.\exists y.f(x_e) \wedge g(y_a) \wedge arg1(x_e, y_a)$$

  unlike its predecessor, UDepLambda¬ allows for nested dependencies between parent and child node which is necessary to model scope phenomena.

- In cases such as the sub-expression (neg 'John does eat' not), the edge label neg and the word 'not' carry the exact same semantics (i.e. the negation operator $\neg$). For these *functional words* we try to define semantics on the dependency edges only rather than on the word. As shown below, reducing Q does not impact the semantic composition of the edge neg:

$$neg := \lambda P.\lambda Q.\lambda f.\neg P(\lambda x.f(x))$$
$$not := \lambda f.TRUE$$

Composition. The lambda expressions are reduced by following the traversal order decided during the *binarization* step. Let's exemplify the composition step by showing at the same time how **simple verbal negation** composes semantically, where the input s-expression is (neg (aux ($nsubj$ eat John) does) not). The substitution step assigns vertices and edges the following semantics:

'eat' $:= \lambda f.\exists x.eat(x_e) \wedge f(x)$
'not' $:= \lambda f.TRUE$
'John' $:= \lambda f.\exists x.named(x_a, John, PER) \wedge f(x)$
'does' $:= \lambda f.TRUE$

$$nsubj := \lambda P.\lambda Q.\lambda f.P(\lambda x.f(x) \wedge Q(\lambda y.Actor(x_e, y_a)))$$
$$aux := \lambda P.\lambda Q.\lambda f.P(\lambda x.f(x))$$
$$neg := \lambda P.\lambda Q.\lambda f.\neg P(\lambda x.f(x))$$
$$ex\text{-}closure := \lambda x.TRUE$$

where the subscripts e and a stands for the event-type and the individual-type existential variable respectively. As for the edge neg, the child of a aux edge is ignored because not contributing to the overall semantics of the sentence.[2] We start by reducing (neg eat not), where P is the parent vertex 'eat' and Q the child vertex 'not'. This yields the expression:[3]

$$\lambda f.\neg \exists x.eat(x_e) \wedge f(x)$$

We then use this logic form to first reduce the lambda expression on the edge aux, which outputs the same input representation, and then compose this with the semantics of the edge $nsubj$. The final representation of the sentence (after we apply existential closure) is as follows:

$$\neg \exists x.\exists y.eat(x_e) \wedge named(y_a, John, PER) \wedge Actor(x_e, y_a)$$

Given the resulting logical form we consider as part of negation scope all the material under the negation operator $\neg$.

4 Analysis of negative constructions

4.1 The quantifier 'no'

Let's consider the sentence 'No man came' along with its dependency trees and logical form, shown in Figure 3.

As shown in Figure 3(b), one shortcoming of the original UDepLambda is that it doesn't cover universal quantification. However, even if we were to assign any of the following lambda expressions containing material implication to the neg edge connecting parent-λf ('man') and child-λg ('no'):

$$?\lambda f.\lambda g.\lambda x.f(x) \rightarrow \neg f(x)$$
$$?\lambda f.\lambda g.\lambda x.f(x) \rightarrow g(x)$$

the resulting expressions would have no means of later accommodating the event 'came' in the consequent of the material implication:

$$*\lambda x.man(x) \rightarrow \neg man(x)$$
$$*\lambda x.man(x) \rightarrow no(x)$$

---

[2] The present work does not consider the semantics of time the word 'does' might contribute to.

[3] Step-by-step derivations are shown in Appendix A.

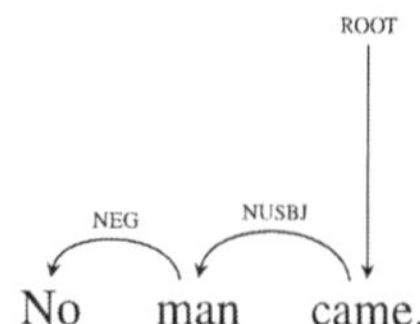

(a) Original UD Dependency Tree

$$\exists x.came(x_e) \wedge \neg\exists y.man(y_a) \wedge arg1(x_e, y_a)$$

(b) UDepLambda Logical Form

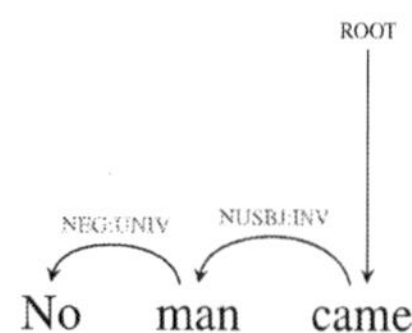

(c) Enhanced UD Dependency Tree

$$\forall y.man(y_a) \rightarrow \neg\exists x.came(x_e) \wedge Actor(x_e, y_a)$$

(d) Desired Logical Form

Figure 3: The dependency trees for 'No man came' (top: original UD tree; bottom: enhanced UD tree) and its logical forms

The higher-order type theory of UDepLambda¬ solves this problem by ensuring that a) there is a universal quantified variable along with material implication and b) the entity bound to it ($man(x)$) is introduced only in the antecedent, whereas the negated event (along with other arguments) only in the consequent. The lambda expression assigned to the *neg* edge is the following

$$\lambda P.\lambda Q.\lambda f.\forall x.(P(\lambda y.EQ(x,y)) \rightarrow \neg f(x))$$

where f allows to leave a 'handle' for the event 'came' to be further composed in the subsequent only, whereas the two-place function $EQ(x,y)$ as argument of P binds the word in the parent node with the universally quantified variable x.

It is worth mentioning at this point that although the universal quantifier 'no' is parsed as depending from an edge *neg*, it possesses a semantics that distinguishes it from other negative adverbs such as 'not' or 'never', in the fact that they bind their head to a universally quantifiable

variable. In these cases we also *enhance* the label on the dependency edge to reflect this more fine-grained distinction. In the presence of 'no' the *neg* edge becomes **neg:univ** if its child vertex is a universal quantifier. This edit operation relies on having a list of lexical items for both universal quantifiers and negation cues in a language, which is easily obtainable given that these items form a small, closed class.

A further edit operation is needed to make sure that the quantifier always outscopes the negation operator; to do so, we modify the semantics of the edge that connects the head of the edge *neg:univ* ('man') with its parent ('came'), *nsubj*, by inverting the order of the Q and P, so that the former outscopes the latter. We call this enhanced edge an '*edge-name*:inv.' edge. Compared to *nsubj*, the semantics of **nsubj:inv** would be as follows:

$$nsubj :=$$
$$\lambda P.\lambda Q.\lambda f.P(\lambda x.f(x) \wedge Q(\lambda y.Actor(x_e, y_a)))$$
$$nsubj\text{-}inv :=$$
$$\lambda P.\lambda Q.\lambda f.Q(\lambda y.P(\lambda x.Actor(x_e, y_a) \wedge f(x)))$$

Using the edited input UD graph, the hierarchy we follow during composition is *neg:univ > nsubj:inv* to yield the s-expression (*nsubj:inv* (*neg:univ* no man) came). Given the following input semantics:

$$man := \lambda f.\exists x.man(x_a) \wedge f(x)$$
$$came := \lambda f.\exists x.came(x_e) \wedge f(x)$$
$$neg:univ :=$$
$$\lambda P.\lambda Q.\lambda f.\forall x.(P(\lambda y.EQ(x,y)) \rightarrow \neg f(x))$$
$$nsubj:inv :=$$
$$\lambda P.\lambda Q.\lambda f.Q(\lambda y.P(\lambda x.Actor(x_e, y_a) \wedge f(x)))$$

we first reduce the lambda expression on the edge *neg:univ.* to yield the expression $\lambda f.\forall x.(man(x_a) \rightarrow \neg f(x))$ and then combine it along the edge *nsubj:inv* to yield the following representation:

$$\forall y.(man(y_a) \rightarrow \neg\exists x.came(x_e) \wedge Actor(x_e, y_a))$$

, where the scope of negation is correctly converted as inside the universal quantifier.

Inverting the order of the parent and child nodes in the semantics of the *:inv.* edge always allows to represent the universally quantified element as outscoping the event it depends on. At the same time, all other arguments and modifiers of the parent event will always compose inside the consequent. This applies to our initial example in Figure 1, where composing the s-expression (*dobj:inv.* borders 'no country') to yield the expression:

$$\lambda f.\forall y.(country(y_a) \to$$
$$\neg\exists x.borders(x_e) \wedge Theme(x_e, y_a) \wedge f(x))$$

, makes sure that further material can only be added in place of $f(e)$, which is inside the scope of $\neg$, in turn in the scope of $\forall$. So when composing the semantics of the subject 'Malta' $(:= \lambda f.\exists x.named(x_a, Malta, ORG) \wedge f(x))$, the universal will still have wide-scope, as shown below:

$$\forall y.(country(y_a) \to$$
$$\neg\exists x.\exists z.named(z_a, Malta, PER) \wedge$$
$$borders(x_e z) \wedge Theme(x_e, y_a) \wedge Actor(x_e, z_a))$$

4.2 Negation and universal quantifier

Alongside quantifiers inherently expressing negation, as the one shown in the previous section, another challenging scope representation arises during the interaction between a negation cue and a non-negative universal quantifier, such 'every'. Let's take as example the sentences 'Not every man came', shown in Figure 4 alongside its FOL representation.

If compared to the representation of the sentence 'No man came', where the universal quantifier outscopes the negation operator, the construction 'not every' yields the opposite interaction where the quantifier is in the scope of $\neg$ (correspondent to the meaning 'there exists some man who came').

As shown in the previous section and here in Figure 4(b), UDepLambda cannot deal with such constructions, yielding a meaning where there exists and event but there doesn't exists the entity that performs it. On the other hand, UDepLambda¬ can easily derive the correct representation by applying the same edits to the UD graph shown in the previous section. First, we enhance the *det* edge to become a more fine-grained *det:univ* in the presence of the child node 'every'. Second, we change *nsubj* into *nsubj-inv.*, since a universal quantifier is in its yield. The lambda expression assigned to the edge *det:univ* is as follows:

$$det:univ := \lambda P.\lambda Q.\lambda f.\forall x.(P(\lambda y. EQ(x,y)) \to f(x))$$

Once again, we deploy the usual bottom-up binarization hierarchy where all modifiers of a head need to be composed before the head itself can be used for further composition. In the case of 'not every...', we start from the modifiers 'every'

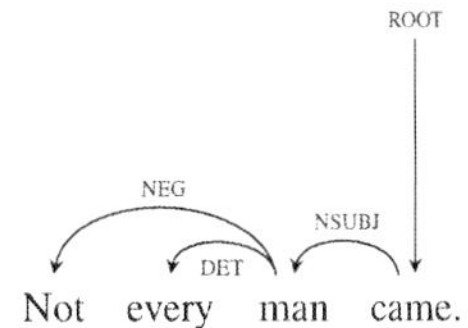

(a) UD tree

$$\lambda f.\lambda g.\lambda x.came(x_e) \wedge arg1(x_e, y_a) \wedge$$
$$\neg\exists y.man(y_a) \wedge every(y_a)$$

(b) UDepLambda Logical Form

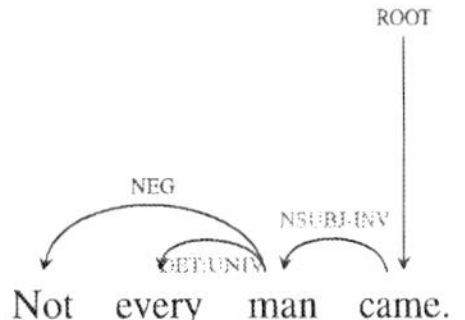

(c) Enhanced UD tree

$$\neg\forall y.(man(y_a) \to \exists x.came(x_e) \wedge Actor(x_e, y_a))$$

(d) Desidered Logical Form

(*nsubj-inv.* came (*neg* (*univ* man every) not))

(e) S-Expression

Figure 4: The sentence 'Not every man came' along with its dependency trees and logical forms

and 'not' and compose the edges following the order *det:univ* ⟩ *neg* so to make sure that negation operator $\neg$ outscopes the universal quantifier $\forall$. After the modifiers of the head 'man' are composed, we can then move on to compose the head itself with its governor node, the event 'came'. The *nsubj:inv.* edge ensures that the subject scopes over the event and not the other way around. Following this, we are able to obtain the final representation:

$$\neg\forall y.(man(y_a) \to \exists x.came(x_e) \wedge Actor(x_e, y_a))$$

4.3 Nobody/nothing/nowhere

As shown in Table 1, 'nobody', 'nothing' and 'nowhere' belong to that class of negation cues whose parent edge do not mark them as inherently expressing negation. However using an hand-crafted list of negation cues for English, we can detect and assign them the semantic representation $\lambda f.\neg\exists x.thing/person/location(x_a) \wedge f(x)$, where the negation operator scopes over an existentially bound entity.

Binarization and composition vary according to

	nobody	nothing	nowhere
nsubj	7	18	-
dobj	-	34	-
conj	-	8	-
nsubjpass	1	6	-
root	-	8	-
advmod	-	-	3
nmod	-	4	-
other	-	8	-
tot.	8	86	3

Table 1: Distribution of nobody, nothing and nowhere with their related dependency tags as they appear in the English UD corpus (McDonald et al., 2013)

whether these elements are arguments or adjuncts. If an argument, the scope of negation includes also the event, otherwise the latter is excluded. To this end, let's compare the sentences 'Nobody came' and 'John came with nothing', along with their dependency graphs and logic forms (Figure 5).

The argument 'nobody' in 'Nobody came' yields a scope reading where the negation operator scopes over the existential. To achieve such reading we once again convert the *nsubj* (or any argument edge for that matter) into a *nsubj:inv.* edge. This is reminiscent of how we handled universal quantification when we introduced the quantifier 'no', which is in fact integral part of such lexical elements (the semantics of '*no*-body came' can be in fact read as 'for all x such that x is a person that x did not come'). Also, the fact that the semantics of these elements is represented through an existential and not a universal bound variable is no problem since we are working under the equivalence $\forall x.P(x) \rightarrow \neg Q(x) \equiv \neg \exists x.P(x) \wedge Q(x)$.

Given the s-expression (*nsubj:inv.* came nobody) the composition is then as follows:

$$\neg \exists x.\exists y.person(y_a) \wedge f(x) \wedge Actor(x_e, y_a) \wedge came(x_e)$$

On the other hand, when the negated lexical element is embedded in an adjunct, as in 'with nothing', no enhancement of the original dependency edges takes place since we want to preserve negation scope inside the phrase (so to yield a reading where the event 'John came' did indeed take place). By substituting and combining the semantics of the s-expression (*nmod:with* came nothing), where the edge *nmod:with* is assigned the lambda expression $\lambda P.\lambda Q.\lambda f.P(\lambda x.f(x) \wedge$

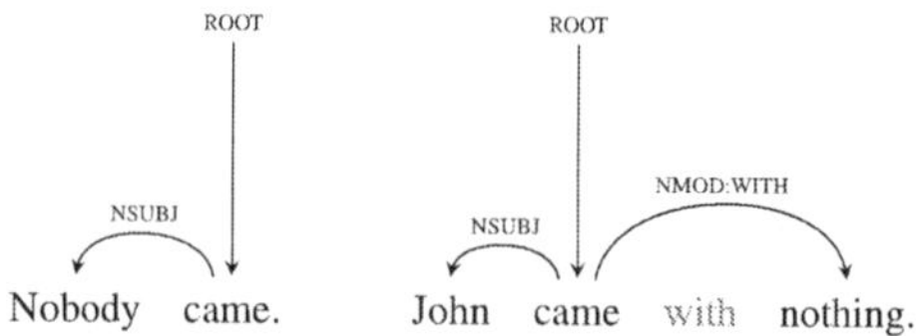

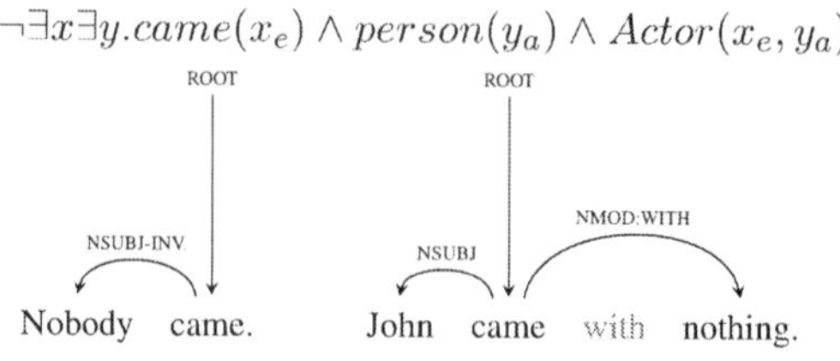

$$\exists x \exists y.came(x_e) \wedge named(y_a, John, PER) \wedge$$
$$Actor(x_e, y_a) \wedge \neg \exists z.thing(z_a) \wedge with(x_e, z_a)$$

Figure 5: Dependency graphs and FOL representations for the sentences 'Nobody came' (above) vs. 'John came with nothing' (below).

$Q(\lambda y.with(x_e, y_a)))$, we obtain the following logic form:

$$\lambda f.\exists x.came(x_e) \wedge f(x) \wedge \neg \exists y.(thing(y_a) \wedge with(x_e, y_a))$$

, where we can the scope of negation is limited to the propositional phrase. Given that the f is outside the scope of negation, further compositions (in the case along the edge *nsubj.*) will also compose outside it, yielding the correct form in Figure (5).

The only limitation we have observed so far concerns 'nowhere' ($:= \lambda f.\exists x.location(x_a) \wedge f(x)$) and the fact it is always associated with a dependency tag *advmod*. The tag *advmod* describes however the manner an action is carried out and has the logical form $\lambda P.\lambda Q.\lambda f.P(\lambda x.f(x) \wedge Q(\lambda y.Manner(x_e, y_a)))$. This is however different from how 'nowhere' is treated in the Groeningen Meaning Bank, where it is described as *where* and not *how* the event takes place. That is, our framework would assign a sentence like 'They got nowhere near the money' the logical form $\exists x.got(x_e) \wedge \neg \exists y.(location(y_a) \wedge Manner(x_e, y_a))$, whereas the one contained in the GMB is: $\exists x.got(x_e) \wedge \neg \exists y_a.(location(y_a) \wedge in(x_e, y_a))$

4.4 Further remarks

Building on the principle of relying on dependency label information as much as possible while using minimal lexical information, we showed that UDepLambda¬ is able to deal with complex phenomena involving negation scope. Although the theory is not shown in full here, these phenomena also include **discontinuous scope** and **affixal negation**, which are part of more recent corpora used to train systems for detecting negation scope at a *string level* (Morante and Daelemans, 2012).

The ability of dealing with discontinuous scope spans, such as in sentences like 'John screamed and did not laugh', where the subject 'John' and the predicate 'did not laugh' are part of the negation scope but 'screamed' is not, comes from the dependency graphs themselves, where we can recover the shared material by means of simple transformation heuristics.[4]

As for affixal negation (e.g. 'John is *impatient*'), one could use a similar heuristics as in the case of 'nobody/nothing/nowhere' where the lexical element is enhanced with the negation operator ('patient':= $\lambda f.\exists x.patient(x_e) \wedge f(x) \longrightarrow \lambda f.\neg \exists x.patient(x_e) \wedge f(x)$). This relies again on bespoke list of words containing an affixal negation cue.

Given that UDepLambda¬ is based on dependency graphs, the primary limitations of our system are how certain phenomena are handled (or better *not* handled) by a dependency parse. This includes multi-word cues such as 'no way' and 'by no means' and the construction 'neither ... nor'.

5   Conclusion and future work

This paper addressed the problem of representing negation scope from universal dependencies by setting the foundations of *UDepLambda¬*, a conversion framework whose high-order type theory is able to deal with complex semantic phenomena related to scope. The conversion processes we presented show that it is possible to rely on dependency edges and additionally to minimal language-dependent lexical information to compose the semantics of negation scope. The fact that this formalism is able to correctly compose the scope for many complex phenomena related to negation scope is promising.

We are currently working on extending this work in two directions:

1. *Automatic framework evaluation*: given the conversion rules presented in this paper, we are planning to automatically convert the UD graphs for the sentences in the GMB so to compare the graph we automatically generate with a gold-standard representation. This would also to identify and quantify the errors of our framework.

2. *Automatic semantic parsing*: given the connection between this framework and the GMB, we would like to explore the possibility of learning the conversion automatically, so not to rely on an hand-crafted hierarchy to decide the order of edge traversal.

References

Valerio Basile, Johan Bos, Kilian Evang, and Noortje Venhuizen. 2012a. Developing a large semantically annotated corpus. In *LREC 2012, Eighth International Conference on Language Resources and Evaluation*.

Valerio Basile, Johan Bos, Kilian Evang, and Noortje Venhuizen. 2012b. Ugroningen: Negation detection with discourse representation structures. In *Proceedings of the First Joint Conference on Lexical and Computational Semantics-Volume 1: Proceedings of the main conference and the shared task, and Volume 2: Proceedings of the Sixth International Workshop on Semantic Evaluation*, pages 301–309. Association for Computational Linguistics.

Johan Bos. 2016. Expressive power of abstract meaning representations. *Computational Linguistics*.

Lucas Champollion. 2011. Quantification and negation in event semantics.

Federico Fancellu, Adam Lopez, and Bonnie Webber. 2016. Neural networks for negation scope detection. In *Proceedings of the 54th Annual Meeting of the Association for Computational Linguistics*, volume 1, pages 495–504.

Dan Flickinger, Yi Zhang, and Valia Kordoni. 2012. Deepbank: A dynamically annotated treebank of the wall street journal. In *Proceedings of the 11th International Workshop on Treebanks and Linguistic Theories*, pages 85–96.

Hans Kamp, Josef Van Genabith, and Uwe Reyle. 2011. Discourse representation theory. In *Handbook of philosophical logic*, pages 125–394. Springer.

Montserrat Marimon. 2010. The spanish resource grammar. In *LREC*.

Ryan T McDonald, Joakim Nivre, Yvonne Quirmbach-Brundage, Yoav Goldberg, Dipanjan Das, Kuzman Ganchev, Keith B Hall, Slav Petrov, Hao Zhang,

---

[4]We are considering substituting such heuristics with the *Enhanced++* version of the Stanford Dependencies (Schuster and Manning, 2016) where implicit relations between content words are made explicit by adding relations and augmenting relation names.

Oscar Täckström, et al. 2013. Universal dependency annotation for multilingual parsing. In *ACL (2)*, pages 92–97.

Roser Morante and Walter Daelemans. 2012. Conandoyle-neg: Annotation of negation in conan doyle stories. In *Proceedings of the Eighth International Conference on Language Resources and Evaluation, Istanbul*. Citeseer.

Woodley Packard, Emily M Bender, Jonathon Read, Stephan Oepen, and Rebecca Dridan. 2014. Simple negation scope resolution through deep parsing: A semantic solution to a semantic problem. In *ACL (1)*, pages 69–78.

Siva Reddy, Oscar Täckström, Michael Collins, Tom Kwiatkowski, Dipanjan Das, Mark Steedman, and Mirella Lapata. 2016. Transforming dependency structures to logical forms for semantic parsing. *Transactions of the Association for Computational Linguistics*, 4:127–140.

Siva Reddy, Oscar Täckström, Slav Petrov, Mark Steedman, and Mirella Lapata. 2017. Universal semantic parsing. *arXiv Preprint*.

Sebastian Schuster and Christopher D Manning. 2016. Enhanced english universal dependencies: An improved representation for natural language understanding tasks. In *Proceedings of the Tenth International Conference on Language Resources and Evaluation (LREC 2016)*.

Erik Velldal, Lilja Øvrelid, Jonathon Read, and Stephan Oepen. 2012. Speculation and negation: Rules, rankers, and the role of syntax. *Computational linguistics*, 38(2):369–410.

Veronika Vincze, György Szarvas, Richárd Farkas, György Móra, and János Csirik. 2008. The bioscope corpus: biomedical texts annotated for uncertainty, negation and their scopes. *BMC bioinformatics*, 9(11):S9.

A Step-by-step λ-reductions

*Throughout the derivations, we are going to use the variable e in place of x_e and z,y or x in place of x_a. Due to space restrictions, we skip reduction for existential closure ($\rightarrow_{ex-clos}$).

A.1 'John does not eat'

$\lambda P.\lambda Q.\lambda f.P(\lambda e.f(e) \wedge Q(\lambda x.Actor(e,x)))(\lambda f.\exists e.eat(e) \wedge f(e))$

$\rightarrow_{\alpha} \lambda P.\lambda Q.\lambda f.P(\lambda e.f(e) \wedge Q(\lambda x.Actor(e,x)))(\lambda g.\exists e'.eat(e') \wedge g(e'))$

$\rightarrow_{\beta} \lambda Q.\lambda f.\lambda g.[\exists e'.eat(e') \wedge g(e')](\lambda e.f(e) \wedge Q(\lambda x.Actor(e,x)))$

$\rightarrow_{\beta} \lambda Q.\lambda f.\exists e'.eat(e') \wedge \lambda e.[f(e) \wedge Q(\lambda x.Actor(e,x))](e')$

$\rightarrow_{\beta} \lambda Q.\lambda f.\exists e'.eat(e') \wedge f(e') \wedge Q(\lambda x.Actor(e',x))$

$\rightarrow_{\beta} \lambda Q.\lambda f.\exists e'.eat(e') \wedge f(e') \wedge Q[\lambda x.Actor(e',x)](\lambda f.\exists x.named(x,John,PER) \wedge f(x))$

$\rightarrow_{\alpha} \lambda Q.\lambda f.\exists e'.eat(e') \wedge f(e') \wedge Q[\lambda x.Actor(e',x)](\lambda g.\exists z.named(z,John,PER) \wedge g(z))$

$\rightarrow_{\beta} \lambda f.\exists e'.eat(e') \wedge f(e') \wedge \lambda g.[\exists z.named(z,John,PER) \wedge g(z)](\lambda x.Actor(e',x))$

$\rightarrow_{\beta} \lambda f.\exists e'.eat(e') \wedge f(e') \wedge \exists z.named(z,John,PER) \wedge \lambda x.[Actor(e',x)](z)$

$\rightarrow_{\beta} \lambda f.\exists e'.eat(e') \wedge f(e') \wedge \exists z.named(z,John,PER) \wedge Actor(e',z)$

$\lambda P.\lambda Q.\lambda f.\neg P(\lambda e.f(e))(\lambda f.\exists e'.\exists z.eat(e') \wedge f(e') \wedge named(z,John,PER) \wedge Actor(e',z))$

$\rightarrow_{\alpha} \lambda P.\lambda Q.\lambda f.\neg P(\lambda e.f(e))(\lambda g.\exists e'.\exists z.eat(e') \wedge g(e') \wedge named(z,John,PER) \wedge Actor(e',z))$

$\rightarrow_{\beta} \lambda Q.\lambda f.\neg\lambda g.[\exists e'.\exists z.eat(e') \wedge g(e') \wedge named(z,John,PER) \wedge Actor(e',z)](\lambda e.f(e))$

$\rightarrow_{\beta} \lambda Q.\lambda f.\neg\exists e'.\exists z.eat(e') \wedge \lambda e.[f(e)](e') \wedge named(z,John,PER) \wedge Actor(e',z)$

$\rightarrow_{\beta} \lambda Q.\lambda f.\neg\exists e'.\exists z.eat(e') \wedge f(e') \wedge named(z,John,PER) \wedge Actor(e',z)$

$\rightarrow_{\beta} \lambda f.\neg\exists e'.\exists z.eat(e') \wedge f(e') \wedge named(z,John,PER) \wedge Actor(e',z)$

$\rightarrow_{\beta} \lambda f.[\neg\exists e'.\exists z.eat(e') \wedge named(z,John,PER) \wedge Actor(e',z) \wedge f(e')](\lambda x.TRUE)$

$\rightarrow_{\beta} \neg\exists e'.\exists z.eat(e') \wedge named(z,John,PER) \wedge Actor(e',z) \wedge \lambda x.[TRUE](e')$

$\rightarrow_{\beta} \mathbf{\neg\exists e'.\exists z.eat(e') \wedge named(z,John,PER) \wedge Actor(e',z)}$

A.2 'No man came'

$\lambda P.\lambda Q.\lambda f.\forall x.(P(\lambda y.EQ(x,y)) \rightarrow \neg f(x))(\lambda f.\exists x.man(x) \wedge f(x))$

$\rightarrow_{\alpha} \lambda P.\lambda Q.\lambda f.\forall x.(P(\lambda y.EQ(x,y)) \rightarrow \neg f(x))(\lambda f'.\exists z.man(z) \wedge f'(z))$

$\rightarrow_{\beta} \lambda Q.\lambda f.\forall x.(\lambda f'.[\exists z.man(z) \wedge f'(z)](\lambda y.EQ(x,y)) \rightarrow \neg f(x))$

$\rightarrow_{\beta} \lambda Q.\lambda f.\forall x.(\exists z.man(z) \wedge \lambda y.[EQ(x,y)](z) \rightarrow \neg f(x))$

$\rightarrow_{\beta} \lambda Q.\lambda f.\forall x.(\exists z.man(z) \wedge EQ(x,z) \rightarrow \neg f(x))$

$\rightarrow_{EQ} \lambda Q.\lambda f.\forall x.(man(x) \rightarrow \neg f(x))$

$\rightarrow_{\beta} \lambda f.\forall x.(man(x) \rightarrow \neg f(x))$

$\lambda P.\lambda Q.\lambda f.Q(\lambda x.P(\lambda e.Actor(e,x) \wedge f(e)))(\lambda f.\exists e.came(e) \wedge f(e))$

$\rightarrow_{\alpha} \lambda P.\lambda Q.\lambda f.Q(\lambda x.P(\lambda e.Actor(e,x) \wedge f(e)))(\lambda g.\exists e'.came(e') \wedge g(e'))$

$\rightarrow_{\beta} \lambda Q.\lambda f.Q(\lambda x.\lambda g.[\exists e'.came(e') \wedge g(e')](\lambda e.Actor(e,x) \wedge f(e)))$

$\rightarrow_{\beta} \lambda Q.\lambda f.Q(\lambda x.\exists e'.came(e') \wedge \lambda e.[Actor(e,x) \wedge f(e)](e'))$

$\rightarrow_{\beta} \lambda Q.\lambda f.Q(\lambda x.\exists e'.came(e') \wedge Actor(e',x) \wedge f(e'))$

$\rightarrow_{\alpha} \lambda Q.\lambda f.Q(\lambda x.\exists e'.came(e') \wedge Actor(e',x) \wedge f(e'))(\lambda f'.\forall x'.(man(x') \rightarrow \neg f'(x')))$

$\rightarrow_{\beta} \lambda f.\lambda f'.[\forall x'.(man(x') \rightarrow \neg f'(x'))](\lambda x.\exists e'.came(e') \wedge Actor(e',x) \wedge f(e'))$

$\rightarrow_{\beta} \lambda f.\forall x'.(man(x') \rightarrow \neg\lambda x.[\exists e'.came(e') \wedge Actor(e',x) \wedge f(e')](x'))$

$\rightarrow_{\beta} \lambda f.\forall x'.(man(x') \rightarrow \neg\exists e'.came(e') \wedge Actor(e',x') \wedge f(e'))$

$\rightarrow_{ex-clos} \mathbf{\forall x'.(man(x') \rightarrow \neg\exists e'.came(e') \wedge Actor(e',x'))}$

A.3 'Not every man came'

$\rightarrow_{\forall} \lambda f.\forall x.(man(x) \rightarrow f(x))$

$\rightarrow_{\neg} \lambda f.\neg\forall z.(man(z) \rightarrow f(z))$

$\lambda P.\lambda Q.\lambda f.Q(\lambda x.P(\lambda e.Actor(e,x) \wedge f(e)))(\lambda f.\exists e.came(e) \wedge f(e))$

$\rightarrow_\alpha \lambda P.\lambda Q.\lambda f.Q(\lambda x.P(\lambda e.Actor(e,x) \wedge f(e)))(\lambda g.\exists e'.came(e') \wedge g(e'))$

$\rightarrow_\beta \lambda Q.\lambda f.Q(\lambda x.\lambda g.[\exists e'.came(e') \wedge g(e')](\lambda e.Actor(e,x) \wedge f(e)))$

$\rightarrow_\beta \lambda Q.\lambda f.Q(\lambda x.\exists e'.came(e') \wedge \lambda e.[Actor(e,x) \wedge f(e)](e'))$

$\rightarrow_\beta \lambda Q.\lambda f.Q(\lambda x.\exists e'.came(e') \wedge Actor(e',x) \wedge f(e'))$

$\lambda Q.\lambda f.Q(\lambda x.\exists e'.came(e') \wedge Actor(e',x) \wedge f(e'))(\lambda f.\neg \forall z.(man(z) \rightarrow f(z))$

$\rightarrow_\alpha \lambda Q.\lambda f.Q(\lambda x.\exists e'.came(e') \wedge Actor(e',x) \wedge f(e'))(\lambda f'.\neg \forall z.(man(z) \rightarrow f'(z))$

$\rightarrow_\beta \lambda f.\lambda f'.[\neg \forall z.(man(z) \rightarrow f'(z))](\lambda x.\exists e'.came(e') \wedge Actor(e',x) \wedge f(e'))$

$\rightarrow_\beta \lambda f.\neg \forall z.(man(z) \rightarrow \lambda x.[\exists e'.came(e') \wedge Actor(e',x) \wedge f(e')](z))$

$\rightarrow_\beta \lambda f.\neg \forall z.(man(z) \rightarrow \exists e'.came(e') \wedge Actor(e',z) \wedge f(e'))$

$\rightarrow_{ex-clos.} \neg \forall \mathbf{z}.(\mathbf{man(z)} \rightarrow \exists e'.\mathbf{came(e')} \wedge \mathbf{Actor(e',z)})$

A.4 'Nobody came'

$\lambda P.\lambda Q.\lambda f.Q(\lambda x.P(\lambda e.f(e) \wedge Actor(e,x)))(\lambda f.\exists e.f(e) \wedge came(e))$

$\rightarrow_\alpha \lambda P.\lambda Q.\lambda f.Q(\lambda x.P(\lambda e.f(e) \wedge Actor(e,x)))(\lambda g.\exists e'.g(e') \wedge came(e'))$

$\rightarrow_\beta \lambda Q.\lambda f.Q(\lambda x.\lambda g.[\exists e'.g(e') \wedge came(e')](\lambda e.f(e) \wedge Actor(e,x)))$

$\rightarrow_\beta \lambda Q.\lambda f.Q(\lambda x.\exists e'.\lambda e.[f(e) \wedge Actor(e,x)](e') \wedge came(e'))$

$\rightarrow_\beta \lambda Q.\lambda f.Q(\lambda x.\exists e'.f(e') \wedge Actor(e',x) \wedge came(e'))$

$\lambda Q.\lambda f.Q(\lambda x.\exists e'.f(e') \wedge Actor(e',x) \wedge came(e'))(\lambda f.\neg \exists x.person(x) \wedge f(x))$

$\rightarrow_\alpha \lambda Q.\lambda f.Q(\lambda x.\exists e'.f(e') \wedge Actor(e',x) \wedge came(e'))(\lambda g.\neg \exists z.person(z) \wedge g(z))$

$\rightarrow_\beta \lambda f.\lambda g.[\neg \exists z.person(z) \wedge g(z)](\lambda x.\exists e'.f(e') \wedge Actor(e',x) \wedge came(e'))$

$\rightarrow_\beta \lambda f.\neg \exists z.person(z) \wedge \lambda x.[\exists e'.f(e') \wedge Actor(e',x) \wedge came(e')](z)$

$\rightarrow_\beta \lambda f.\neg \exists z.\exists e'.person(z) \wedge f(e') \wedge Actor(e',z) \wedge came(e')$

$\rightarrow_{ex-clos.} \neg \exists \mathbf{z}.\exists e'.\mathbf{person(z)} \wedge \mathbf{Actor(e',z)} \wedge \mathbf{came(e')}$

A.5 'John came with nothing'

$\lambda P.\lambda Q.\lambda f.P(\lambda e.f(e) \wedge Q(\lambda x.with(e,x)))(\lambda f.\exists e.came(e) \wedge f(e))$

$\rightarrow_\alpha \lambda P.\lambda Q.\lambda f.P(\lambda e.f(e) \wedge Q(\lambda x.with(e,x)))(\lambda g.\exists e'.came(e') \wedge g(e'))$

$\rightarrow_\beta \lambda Q.\lambda f.\lambda g.[\exists e'.came(e') \wedge g(e')](\lambda e.f(e) \wedge Q(\lambda x.with(e,x)))$

$\rightarrow_\beta \lambda Q.\lambda f.\exists e'.came(e') \wedge f(e') \wedge \lambda e.[Q(\lambda x.with(e,x))](e')$

$\rightarrow_\beta \lambda Q.\lambda f.\exists e'.came(e') \wedge f(e') \wedge Q(\lambda x.with(e',x))$

$\rightarrow_\beta \lambda Q.\lambda f.\exists e'.came(e') \wedge f(e') \wedge Q[\lambda x.with(e',x)](\lambda f.\neg \exists x.thing(x) \wedge f(x))$

$\rightarrow_\alpha \lambda Q.\lambda f.\exists e'.came(e') \wedge f(e') \wedge Q[\lambda x.with(e',x)](\lambda g.\neg \exists z.thing(z) \wedge g(z))$

$\rightarrow_\beta \lambda f.\exists e'.came(e') \wedge f(e') \wedge \lambda g.[\neg \exists z.thing(z) \wedge g(z)](\lambda x.with(e',x))$

$\rightarrow_\beta \lambda f.\exists e'.came(e') \wedge f(e') \wedge \neg \exists z.thing(z) \wedge \lambda x.[with(e',x)](z)$

$\rightarrow_\beta \lambda f.\exists e'.came(e') \wedge f(e') \wedge \neg \exists z.thing(z) \wedge with(e',z)$

$\lambda P.\lambda Q.\lambda f.P(\lambda e.f(e) \wedge Q(\lambda x.Actor(e,x)))(\lambda f.\exists e'.came(e') \wedge f(e') \wedge \neg \exists z.thing(z) \wedge with(e',z))$

$\rightarrow_\alpha \lambda P.\lambda Q.\lambda f.P(\lambda e.f(e) \wedge Q(\lambda x.Actor(e,x)))(\lambda g.\exists e'.came(e') \wedge g(e') \wedge \neg \exists z.thing(z) \wedge with(e',z))$

$\rightarrow_\beta \lambda Q.\lambda f.\lambda g.[\exists e'.came(e') \wedge g(e') \wedge \neg \exists z.thing(z) \wedge with(e',z)](\lambda e.f(e) \wedge Q(\lambda x.Actor(e,x)))$

$\rightarrow_\beta \lambda Q.\lambda f.\exists e'.came(e') \wedge \lambda e.[f(e) \wedge Q(\lambda x.Actor(e,x))](e') \wedge \neg \exists z.thing(z) \wedge with(e',z)$

$\rightarrow_\beta \lambda Q.[\lambda f.\exists e'.came(e') \wedge f(e') \wedge Q(\lambda x.Actor(e',x)) \wedge \neg \exists z.thing(z) \wedge with(e',z)]$
$(\lambda g.\exists y.named(y,John,PER) \wedge g(y))$

$\rightarrow_\beta \quad \lambda f.\exists e'.came(e') \wedge f(e') \wedge \lambda g.[\exists y.named(y,John,PER) \wedge g(y)](\lambda x.Actor(e',x)) \wedge \neg \exists z.thing(z) \wedge with(e',z)]$

$\rightarrow_\beta \lambda f.\exists e'.came(e') \wedge f(e') \wedge \exists y.named(y,John,PER) \wedge \lambda x.[Actor(e',x)](y) \wedge \neg \exists z.thing(z) \wedge with(e',z)$

$\rightarrow_\beta \lambda f.\exists e'.came(e') \wedge \exists y.named(y,John,PER) \wedge f(e') \wedge Actor(e',y) \wedge \neg \exists z.thing(z) \wedge with(e',z)$

$\rightarrow_{ex-clos.} \exists e'.\exists \mathbf{y}.\mathbf{came(e')} \wedge \mathbf{named(y,John,PER)} \wedge \mathbf{Actor(e',y)} \wedge \neg \exists \mathbf{z}.\mathbf{thing(z)} \wedge \mathbf{with(e',z)}$

Meaning Banking beyond Events and Roles
Invited talk

Johan Bos
University of Groningen
`johan.bos@rug.nl`

Abstract

In this talk I will discuss the analysis of several semantic phenomena that need meaning representations that can describe attributes of propositional contexts. I will do this in a version of Discourse Representation Theory, using a universal semantic tagset developed as part of a project that aims to produce a large meaning bank (a semantically-annotated corpus) for four languages (English, Dutch, German and Italian).

Proceedings of the Workshop Computational Semantics Beyond Events and Roles (SemBEaR), page 33,
Valencia, Spain, April 4, 2017. ©2017 Association for Computational Linguistics

The Scope and Focus of Negation:
A Complete Annotation Framework for Italian

Begoña Altuna
University of the Basque Country
(UPV/EHU), Spain
begona.altuna@ehu.eus

Anne-Lyse Minard   Manuela Speranza
Fondazione Bruno Kessler (FBK),
Trento, Italy
minard,manspera@fbk.eu

Abstract

In this paper we present a complete framework for the annotation of negation in Italian, which accounts for both negation scope and negation focus, and also for language-specific phenomena such as negative concord. In our view, the annotation of negation complements more comprehensive Natural Language Processing tasks, such as temporal information processing and sentiment analysis. We applied the proposed framework and the guidelines built on top of it to the annotation of written texts, namely news articles and tweets, thus producing annotated data for a total of over 36,000 tokens.

1   Introduction

The digital era has enabled the creation of large amounts of data that can be used in many knowledge fields. These data, however, need to be "understood" to be useful. Natural Language Processing (NLP) aims at analyzing and extracting textual information that can be employed in tasks such as decision making (Demner-Fushman et al., 2009) or event forecasting (Radinsky and Horvitz, 2013) among many others.

The analysis and processing of the negation itself is relevant to areas such as event information processing (Minard et al., 2016), sentiment analysis (Jia et al., 2009) and discourse relation identification (Asr and Demberg, 2015). On the one hand, knowing whether an event is affirmed or negated is of utmost importance in the domain of temporal processing for determining the factuality of an event. The positive or negative polarity of an event, in fact, will determine its factuality value, that is to say, whether an event is said to happen or not. Knowing which part of the sen-

tence is most directly negated, on the other hand, may help discriminate which entities participate in an event, which can be very helpful when building entity-based timelines and storylines (Laparra et al., 2015).

The task of sentiment analysis consists predominantly of determining whether a proposition has a positive or a negative polarity. In this case, the presence of a negation can revert the polarity of the proposition and, thus, its identification is essential. Finally in the domain of discourse analysis, the analysis of the expression of negation is needed when extracting relations between parts of the discourse, for example to find *chose alternative* relations or *contrast* constructions.

While affirmative sentences do not need any syntactic marker, negation is typically expressed by some kind of syntactic or lexical element that changes the polarity of the whole sentence or of some elements of the sentence. Each language has its own means to express negation. Therefore, these have to be identified and their features analyzed as a preliminary step towards the completion of an annotation framework.

We propose a complete annotation framework for the annotation of negation in Italian built on the work by Morante et al. (2011) and Blanco and Moldovan (2011). In our framework the semantics of negation is represented through the identification of the negation cue (i.e. the lexical element expressing negation), its scope (i.e. the text section that is negated), its focus (i.e. that part of the scope that is prominently or explicitly negated) and, if present, its reinforcement (i.e. an auxiliary negation). In (1) we give an example of negation and its annotation[1]. The novelty of our framework

---

[1]In our examples we will use the following notational conventions: if marked, a negation cue will be highlighted in bold, its reinforcement will be in italics, its focus will be included in square brackets and its scope will be underlined.

Proceedings of the Workshop Computational Semantics Beyond Events and Roles (SemBEaR), pages 34–42,
Valencia, Spain, April 4, 2017. ©2017 Association for Computational Linguistics

lies in considering all at once the annotation of the scope and the focus of a negation, which implies making some adaptation of the annotation of one with regard to the other.

(1) **Non** ha parlato [con loro].
     (He didn't speak with them.)

We applied this annotation framework on sample sentences taken from written news articles and produced detailed annotation guidelines[2]. Finally, following these annotation guidelines, we annotated two different typologies of written texts, i.e. news articles and tweets, for a total of over 36,000 tokens.

The paper is divided as follows: in Section 2 we summarize the related work on negation annotation, in Section 3 we highlight the main features of the proposed annotation framework, in Section 4 we provide details about the annotation effort we have conducted and in Section 5 we explain how our annotation can be useful for other NLP tasks. Finally, in Section 6 we discuss future work.

2   Related Work

Many annotation efforts on negation have been conducted in recent years for different purposes. Some of the first attempts of negation annotation were done in biomedical text corpora for which annotation guidelines for negation were created. On one hand, the GENIA corpus manual (Kim et al., 2006) was employed for the annotation of GE-NIA (Kim et al., 2008), a corpus of 1,000 abstracts annotated with negated biological events and three levels of uncertainty. On the other hand, the BioInfer annotation scheme (Pyysalo et al., 2007) was used for the annotation of entities and the relations and dependencies among them in the BioInfer corpus. The absence of such relationships as in "not affected by" or "independent of" was annotated with the special predicate *NOT*.

The biomedical corpus BioScope (Vincze et al., 2008) is the first corpus in which negation was specifically targeted; it consists of 20,000 sentences, 13% of which contain some negative expression. BioScope is annotated not only with negation cues but also with negation scope, whose

extent is defined as the largest syntactic unit possible.

The guidelines followed in the annotation of the BioScope corpus have been adapted to different domains. Morante et al. (2011), for example, focused on narrative texts and defined the annotation of negated events in addition to negation cues and their scope. Following this, Morante and Daelemans (2012) created and released the ConanDoyle-neg corpus, a corpus containing Sherlock Holmes' stories annotated with negation and event information, as well as coreference, semantic roles and implicit arguments. In addition, a further adaptation of the BioScope guidelines has been used to annotate the SFU Review Corpus (Konstantinova et al., 2012), a corpus consisting of 400 customer reviews.

PropBank (Palmer et al., 2005) also contains negation information: a *NEG* functional tag has been assigned to the modifiers expressing negation such as "not", "n't", "never" and "no longer", as defined in the PropBank guidelines (Bonial et al., 2010). On top of this annotation Blanco and Moldovan (2011) marked the focus of the negation, defined as the most directly and explicitly negated part of the sentence. The resulting dataset was employed, together with the ConanDoyle-neg corpus, in the *SEM 2012 Shared Task *Resolving the Scope and Focus of Negation*[3].

Among corpora containing annotations of negation and its scope it is worth mentioning the Product Review Corpus (Councill et al., 2010), which was built automatically with a system trained on the BioScope corpus.

While the work mentioned above focuses exclusively on the English language, the only work on negation in Italian we are aware of is that of Attardi et al. (2015) in the medical domain. They annotated a corpus of medical records in Italian with medical entities (diseases, drugs, etc.) and added a marker to indicate whether an entity appears in a negative context. This annotation is limited to the identification of the absence or presence of a medical entity.

However, Spanish and Italian are closely related languages and share many features, which allowed us to take into consideration work on negation in Spanish. Similar to the work on Italian medical records, Stricker et al. (2015) have anno-

---

[2]The guidelines for the annotation of negation cues, focus and scope in Italian are not public yet, as we are still improving the document in terms of clarity of exposition and examples, but is accessible at the following link: `https://goo.gl/kAmRwN`

[3]`http://www.clips.ua.ac.be/sem2012-st-neg/`

tated radiology reports with findings (observations and medical conditions) and they have assigned a value, "affirmed" or "negated", to each of those findings. More similar to our aim, we can cite the Spanish section of the SFU Review Corpus (Martí et al., 2016), which has been annotated with negation by Jiménez-Zafra et al. (to appear), partially following the ABSA guidelines used for Task 12 in SemEval-2015[4].

3 Annotation Specifications

We propose an annotation scheme for negation in which we have defined the elements to be annotated and their features based on (Morante et al., 2011) and (Blanco and Moldovan, 2011), thus including negation cues, negation scope and focus.

Having Italian as the target language, we relied on the Italian grammar by Serianni and Castelvecchi (1988) and on corpus observation for language-specific phenomena related to negation.

3.1 Negation Cues

Negation is a linguistic phenomenon that inverts the truth value of the proposition it is applied to (Martí et al., 2016). Negation is usually expressed by lexical and syntactic elements that are called negation cues.

Following Morante et al. (2011), only negation cues expressed by adverbs, such as *non* / "not", pronouns, as *nessuno* / "nobody", determiners, as *nessun* / "any", and prepositions, as *senza* / "without" have been taken into consideration in our annotation effort. Negation expressed by verbs or nouns, on the other hand, (as in *Rifiuto* / "I refuse", see example (2)), remains out of our scope. It is also relevant to note that we have not addressed affixal negation (e.g. the negative prefixes *in-* and *a-*, see example 3) as we do not want to go below the unit of a token.

(2)   *Rifiuto* di parlare.
      (I refuse to talk.)

(3)   Un *im*percettibile odore inondava la stanza.
      (An imperceptible smell invaded the room.)

As a result of exhaustive research on negation cues in Italian, we have compiled a list that includes both one-word constructions (e.g *non* /

"not", see example (4)) and multi-word expressions (e.g. *per niente* / "(not) at all", see example (5)).

(4)   Il dato **non** è ancora preciso.
      (The data is not precise yet.)

(5)   Era una donna **per niente** candida.
      (*She was a woman not at all candid.)

Following Morante et al. (2011) we do not annotate as negation cues those negative forms that do not actually express negation, such as the expletive *non* in *non appena* / "as soon as" or *non* in fixed constructions such as *non a caso* / "not by chance".

In general, every negation cue is associated with its scope and focus. Ellipsis, unfinished sentences and other phenomena, however, may prevent it from happening as it is the case of *no* / "no" when it is a one-word answer to a question. In (6), for example, *no* is annotated as a negation cue with no focus or scope as the reference to winning is expressed in the previous sentence, while the annotation of the scope and focus of a negation does not go beyond sentence boundaries.

(6)   Avete vinto? **No.**
      (Did you win? No.)

3.2 Scope

As Morante et al. (2011) do, we consider the scope of a negation cue to be the extent of the text affected by the cue; more specifically, the scope of a negation corresponds to the section of text expressing the proposition whose truth value is inverted by the negation. The suggested test to determine the extent of the scope "it is not the case that" proposed by Morante et al. is also employed for Italian (*non si dà il caso*).

As a general rule, the negation cue remains out of the scope since it does not change its own polarity (7)[5]. However, an innovative feature of our framework is that negation cues which carry a richer semantic meaning than plain negation are included inside the scope; this is the case, among others, of *nessun* / "no (determiner)" (8), *mai* / "never", *nessuno* / "nobody", and *nulla* / "nothing".

We have taken the decision of including such negation cues in the scope because they convey

---

[4]http://alt.qcri.org/semeval2015/task12/

[5]Note that, as a consequence of this, the extent of the scope can be discontinuous, as in (7).

more than just a negative meaning. When turning negative sentences into affirmative sentences, the plain negation cues will be removed whereas richer semantic negation cues will be replaced by a positive counterpart. For example the affirmative version of the sentence (7) will be *Il presidente tratta con gli assassini* / "The president deals with the murderers", and for the sentence (8) *Qualche militare italiano é rimasto ferito* / "Some Italian soldiers have been wounded".

(7) Il presidente **non** tratta con gli assassini.
(The president does not deal with murderers.)

(8) **Nessun** militare italiano è rimasto ferito.
(No Italian soldier has been wounded.)

3.3 Focus

Focus is defined as that part of the scope that is most prominently or explicitly negated (Huddleston and Pullum, 2002); as an example, *con gli assassini* / "with the murderers" is the focus of *non* / "not" in (9).

(9) Il presidente **non** tratta [con gli assassini].
(The president does not deal with murderers.)

In some cases it is possible that the extent of the focus coincides with the negation cue; this happens with negation cues which not only express negation but carry a richer semantic meaning. For example, *mai* / "never" expresses a reference to time, while *nessuno* / "nobody" expresses a reference to human beings (10).

(10) [**Nessuno**] ha cercato di fermare l'uomo.
(Nobody tried to stop the man.)

It is worth underlining that this is perfectly in tune with the decision explained above (Section 3.2) to include these negation cues within the extent of the scope.

3.4 Reinforcement

In Italian (as in other romance languages such as Spanish), negations precede the verb (11 and 12). When the negation is moved after the verb as in (13), an auxiliary negation (reinforcement) is added to fill the position that has been left empty. In this case, we annotate the negation cue and associate it with the reinforcement, besides associating it with its focus and scope as in all other cases.

(11) I militari italiani **non** sono [rimasti feriti].
(Italian soldiers have not been wounded.)

(12) [**Nessun** militare italiano] è rimasto ferito.
(No Italian soldier has been wounded.)

(13) *Non* è rimasto ferito [**nessun** militare italiano].
(No Italian soldier has been wounded.)

3.5 Discussion

In our framework we address both scope and focus. Since, by definition, the focus is the most prominently negated part of the scope, we explicitly added the constraint according to which the focus should always be included in the scope.

In cleft sentences though, the focus is detached from the clause where the negation cue is placed; in (14), for instance, the focus is *dal 30 agosto* / "since the 30th of August". As a result, the focus would be outside the extent of the scope (the annotation of the scope, in fact, does not go over clause boundaries). To ensure that the focus is included within the scope, we decided to expand the extent of the scope to include as well the detached part of the cleft sentence.

(14) È [dal 30 agosto] che **non** si può più comprare.
(It is since the 30th of August that it is no longer possible to buy it.)

The annotation of relative pronouns and the elements they refer to (noun, pronoun or phrase) is also worth a more detailed discussion. In order to be aligned with the annotation framework proposed by Morante et al. (2011), we decided to include relative pronouns in the scope, but not their antecedents. For example, in (15), we have annotated *che hanno voluto andarci* / "who did want to go there" as the scope.

However, one might argue that the inclusion of the antecedents (*i bambini che hanno voluto andarci* / "the children who did want to go there") would have made the scope more informative and that the "it is not the case that" test (see Section 3.2) suggests to include *bambini* / "children" in the scope.

(15) Sono i bambini [**che**] **non** hanno voluto andarci.
(It is the children who did not want to go there.)

4 Annotating Negation

The annotation framework described above has been applied to an annotation task which included two significantly different types of texts, i.e. news articles and tweets.

4.1 Negation in Fact-Ita Bank

We annotated with negation 71 documents of Fact-Ita Bank (Minard et al., 2014), a corpus which consists of 169 news stories taken from Ita-TimeBank (Caselli et al., 2011).

From Ita-TimeBank, it inherited the annotation of events, which was performed following It-TimeML (Caselli et al., 2011), the Italian version of the TimeML annotation scheme.

For a subset of 6,958 events, Fact-Ita Bank contains the annotation of the factuality attributes (i.e. polarity, time and certainty) as defined for FactA - Factuality Annotation (Minard et al., 2016), a task which has been organised in 2016 in the context of the EVALITA evaluation campaign[6]. Fact-Ita Bank has been used as training corpus for FactA and is distributed with a CC-BY-NC license[7].

4.2 Negation in Tweets

We annotated with negation 301 tweets that were used as test set for the FactA pilot task on social media texts (Minard et al., 2016).

Also in this case, the texts contained the annotation of events (following It-TimeML) and of the event factuality attributes (as defined for the FactA task at EVALITA 2016).

4.3 Annotation Task

The annotation task has been performed using CAT[8] (Content Annotation Tool) (Lenzi et al., 2012), a web-based text annotation tool. The annotated data are in an XML-based stand-off format where different annotation layers are stored in separate document sections and are related to each other and to source data through pointers.

Four annotators were involved in the annotation task. We estimate the annotation effort to be ten working days of an expert annotator.

[6]http://www.evalita.it/
[7]http://hlt-nlp.fbk.eu/technologies/
fact-ita-bank
[8]http://dh.fbk.eu/resources/
cat-content-annotation-tool

4.4 Inter-Annotator Agreement

When we had completed a first version of the guidelines we tested the inter-annotator agreement (IAA) with three annotators (who had been involved in the definition of the task) over 8 news articles from Fact-Ita Bank, for a total of 47 negation cues[9] (IAA-1).

We computed the F-measure on the exact match for each annotator pair and for each markable (negation cue, scope and focus). Hripcsak and Rothschild (2005) shows that for tasks in which the number of negative cases is unknown, undefined or very large, inter-annotator agreement can be quantified using the average pairwise F-measure. The first column in Table 1 shows the average of the pairwise F-measure values obtained, which is 0.93, 0.52 and 0.55 for the negation cue, the scope and the focus, respectively.

	IAA - 1	IAA - 2
documents	8	4
# negation cues	47	30
negation cue	0.93	0.98
scope	0.52	0.67
focus	0.55	0.58

Table 1: IAA in terms of average pairwise F-measure.

As we were not completely satisfied with the results, we improved the annotation guidelines and enriched them with examples taken from the dataset used for the first test. Then, in order to evaluate the improvement, we produced a small gold standard (4 news articles from Fact-Ita Bank) annotated by two expert annotators (who had been involved in the previous test) and had it annotated by another person who had the improved version of the guidelines as its only source of information (IAA-2).

The second column in Table 1 shows the results of this experiment in terms of F-measure. The agreement on the annotation of the scope in IAA-2 is much better than in IAA-1, with a average F-measure computed on the strict match close to 0.7 (for the scope) and close to 0.6 (for the focus). Moving to a relaxed match (acceptance of one-word difference when comparing two strings) the average F-measure for the scope increases to 0.85 and for the focus it reaches 0.77.

[9]The number of negation cues was computed after the annotators completed the adjudication.

4.5 Discussion

In total we annotated 71 news articles from Fact-Ita Bank, including those used for the IAA, and 301 tweets. In Table 2 we present a quantitative description of the data. We can observe that the average size of scope and focus is bigger in news than in tweets. This is mainly due to the limitation of characters in tweets and to the writing style, which is closer to oral speech, with very short sentences. Not surprisingly, in both corpora the most frequent negation cue is *non* / "not".

	news articles	tweet corpus
docs	71	301
tokens	31,596	4,920
sentences	1,290	301
tweets/sent. w. neg.	278	59
negation cues	282	71
reinforcement	15	9
average size scopes	9.11	4.69
average size focus	3.2	1.61
non [not]	76%	80%
nessun(o/a) [no/nobody]	6%	3%
nulla/niente [nothing]	4%	8%
senza [without]	6%	4%

Table 2: Quantitative data about the annotated corpora

During the annotation and the inter-annotator agreement phases, we noticed that the annotation of the focus in written texts is a very difficult task, even for humans. Taking into account certain linguistic phenomena can help in interpreting a negative sentence to some extent. For example, the fact that a subject pronoun (which is usually omitted in Italian) is expressed in a sentence indicates that the focus is on the subject itself (e.g. in (16) the focus is on the pronoun *io* / "I"). Word order can also be used to determine the focus of a negation, but prosody is undoubtedly the most useful aspect. Since we work on written texts, and do not have this kind of data, our focus annotation strongly relies on the interpretation of the annotator, which decreases inter-annnotator agreement.

(16) [Io] **non** sono d'accordo che abbiano nominato grand Budapest hotel e il libro della vita
(I don't agree with the fact that they have nominated grand Budapest hotel and The Book of Life)

On the other hand, the annotation of the scope is a more straightforward task. In the first inter-annotator agreement phase the agreement for the scope annotation was low due to some imprecision in the guidelines, as well as small issues in the management of nested annotation by the annotation tool. The main disagreements were related to i) the inclusion or not of the negation cues in the scope, ii) the annotation of cleft sentences, and iii) the treatment of parenthetical texts. However, in the second inter-annotator agreement phase, the disagreements concerned mainly the discourse connectives which should be excluded from the scope but were not excluded by one annotator.

The annotation of tweets enabled us to observe new phenomena in the expression of negation and so to add some annotation rules. The main differences between news articles and tweets are the size of the text, and as a result the amount of context information available, and the style (which in tweets is close to that of oral speech, with the use of slang and sometimes vulgar language). In news articles, sentences are well written and often quite long; usually the reader has all the context needed to understand a piece of information. On the other hand, sentences in tweets are very short and sometimes incomplete. Incompleteness can lead to focus ambiguity and even to the absence of the focus. In (17), for example, there are dots where the focus should be. We decided to annotate the verb that is negated, but one could argue that the dots should be annotated as focus instead or that no focus should be associated with the negation cue.

(17) Il Modena ha fatto vedere buone cose ma **non è** ...
(Modena has shown good stuff but it is not. . .)

(18) #Paritàsessi **non** è [sfoggiare ascelle pelose] o [#pisciare in un imbuto per farlo in piedi].
(* #Equalrights is not showing off hairy armpits or peeing in a funnel to do it standing up.)

Another difference between tweets and news articles is the use of non standard language. In tweets we find abbreviations, repeated words, non alpha-numeric symbols, grammar mistakes, and sometimes missing words. When annotating tweets, for instance, we added to our list a negation cue that we had not found before, *nn*, which stands for *non* / "not". Tweets also contain hashtags which are used to link tweets to some category topics and they can include a negation. For example the hashtag *#Nonbeccomailaporta* / "I never strike the target" could be decomposed and annotated with negation: "mai" will be the negation cue and the focus, "non" the reinforcement and "beccomailaporta" the scope. But at the moment, as the annotation tool does not manage the annotation of units smaller than a token, we do not annotate it. Finally, one tweet contained the only case we found of negation of coordinated phrases (e.g. in (18)).

5 Relevance of Negation Annotation

As mentioned in the introduction, our research on negation is motivated by the interest of employing it for temporal information processing and, more speciically, for the processing of events and their factuality value.

The identification of the scope may help in factuality resolution. In our corpus, which has been previously annotated with temporal information, directly negated events like *uccideranno* / "will kill" (19) are given a negative factuality value. Events like *ha rivendicato* / "has claimed responsibility" in (20), instead, have been given a positive polarity as they are not directly negated. In fact, they have a positive factuality value, although they are implicitly counterfactual, since, in this case no responsibility claim has been done.

(19) **Non** [ucciderano] il nostro futuro.
(They will not kill our future.)

(20) [**Nessuno**] ha rivendicato il sequestro.
(Nobody has claimed responsibility for the hijack.)

In example (20), the event *ha rivendicato* falls under the scope of the negation and its factuality value has changed. Either because the event is directly negated (19) or because an argument of that event is negated (20), the final factuality value of an event will be negative.

However, the scope is not enough to decide on the factuality value of an event. *sequestro* / "hijack" in (20) falls also into the scope extent but it preserves its positive polarity, since it is a subordinated event and the negation affects the main clause. Therefore, we consider scope information to be useful for factuality resolution, but it has to

be complemented by other linguistic information such as sentence structure and argument information.

As far as focus is concerned, we assume that in some cases the identification of the focus may help build entity-based timelines, that is to say, timelines that gather and organize the events in which a certain entity participates. As counterfactual or non-factual events have not happened or will not happen, we will exclude those from the timeline.

When an entity is the focus of the negation, we hold that it does not take part in the event, since it is explicitly negated. As a consequence, that event will not be considered for the timeline of that entity. If we were to build a timeline from example (21) taking "Putin" as the target entity, we should include *ha detto* / "has said" and *essere* / "is" in the timeline. On the contrary, *si è recato* / "has attended" will not appear in the timeline, since it is explicitly mentioned, through the negation of the subject *lui* / "he", that he did not attend the funerals. Finally, the event "funerals" has a factual value (i.e. the funerals took place), but since Putin did not go, they will not appear in Putin's timeline.

(21) Putin ha detto di essere col cuore a Beslan, anche se [lui] **non** si è recato ai funerali.
(Putin said his heart is in Beslan, even though he did not attend the funerals.)

Although we have only worked on news documents, we expect that the processing of negation will also be useful for sentiment analysis (e.g. in movie or book reviews). The identification of negation scope may help in defining the polarity of the events in the scope, which is a highly relevant feature in these kinds of texts.

6 Conclusion

In this paper we presented our work on defining a common annotation framework for scope and focus of negations and the annotation performed on two corpora: Fact-Ita Bank, which is composed of news articles, and a corpus of tweets. We conducted this work on the Italian language but we plan to use the annotation framework to perform annotation in other languages, in particular in Spanish, French and Basque.

The interpretation of negation is an important task for detecting the factuality of events and we now have corpora annotated with both negation and factuality at our disposal. In the short term we expect to conduct a study about the relationship between negation scope and factuality annotation.

As far as focus annotation is concerned, we will use that information for the identification of the directly negated entities in order not to include them in role structures. This information will also be used to improve the entity-based timelines and storylines, keeping the events in which negated entities participate out of candidate events to form the timeline.

Our framework does not include the annotation of negation expressed by verbs or nouns (e.g. *cancel*) and affixal negation (e.g. *illegal*). We plan to include these aspects as well and, consequently, to verify to what extent the current annotation guidelines account for their annotation of scope and focus.

Negation does not always have the same intensity and can be total or partial. Some words increase the intensity of the negation and other reduce it. For example the negation in "not all the students arrived" is partial, whereas in "he did not arrive" the negation is total. For the moment, all these cases are annotated in the same way and the different nuances are not considered, but we intend to add some markers of degree to the negation cues, so as to normalize this information.

Finally, the annotated data will be soon made available from the website of the HLT-NLP group at FBK (`http://hlt-nlp.fbk.eu/`) and used to implement and evaluate a system for negation detection in Italian.

References

Fatemeh Torabi Asr and Vera Demberg. 2015. Uniform information density at the level of discourse relations: Negation markers and discourse connective omission. In *Proceedings of the International Conference on Computation Semantics*, pages 118–128.

Giuseppe Attardi, Vittoria Cozza, and Daniele Sartiano. 2015. Annotation and extraction of relations from italian medical records. In *Proceedings of the 6th Italian Information Retrieval Workshop (IIR 2015)*.

Eduardo Blanco and Dan Moldovan. 2011. Semantic Representation of Negation Using Focus Detection. In *Proceedings of the 49th Annual Meeting of the Association for Computational Linguistics: Human Language Technologies*, pages 581–589, Portland, Oregon, USA, June. Association for Computational Linguistics.

Claire Bonial, Olga Babko-Malaya, Jinho D. Choi, Jena Hwang, and Martha Palmer. 2010. Propbank Annotation Guidelines (Version 3.0). Technical report, Center for Computational Language and Education Research, Institute of Cognitive Science, University of Colorado at Boulder.

Tommaso Caselli, Valentina Bartalesi Lenzi, Rachele Sprugnoli, Emanuele Pianta, and Irina Prodanof. 2011. Annotating Events, Temporal Expressions and Relations in Italian: the It-Timeml Experience for the Ita-TimeBank. In *Proceedings of the 5th Linguistic Annotation Workshop*, pages 143–151, Portland, Oregon, USA, June. Association for Computational Linguistics.

Isaac Councill, Ryan McDonald, and Leonid Velikovich. 2010. What's great and what's not: learning to classify the scope of negation for improved sentiment analysis. In *Proceedings of the Workshop on Negation and Speculation in Natural Language Processing*, pages 51–59, Uppsala, Sweden, July. University of Antwerp.

Dina Demner-Fushman, Wendy W. Chapman, and Clement J. McDonald. 2009. What can natural language processing do for clinical decision support? *Journal of Biomedical Informatics*, 42(5):760 – 772.

George Hripcsak and Adam S. Rothschild. 2005. Technical brief: Agreement, the f-measure, and reliability in information retrieval. *Journal of the American Medical Informatics Association*, 12(3):296–298.

Rodney D. Huddleston and Geoffrey K. Pullum. 2002. *The Cambridge Grammar of the English Language*. Cambridge University Press, April.

Lifeng Jia, Clement Yu, and Weiyi Meng. 2009. The effect of negation on sentiment analysis and retrieval effectiveness. In *Proceedings of the 18th ACM Conference on Information and Knowledge Management*, CIKM '09, pages 1827–1830, New York, NY, USA. ACM.

Salud M. Jiménez-Zafra, Mariona Taulé, M. Teresa Martín-Valdivia, L. Alfonso Ureña-López, and M. Antònia Martí. to appear. SFU ReviewSP-NEG: a Spanish corpus annotated with negation for Sentiment Analysis A Typology of negation patterns. *Language Resources and Evaluation*.

Jin-Dong Kim, Tomoko Ohta, Yuka Tateisi, and Jun'ichi Tsujii. 2006. GENIA corpus manual. Technical report, Tsujiilab, University of Tokyo.

Jin-Dong Kim, Tomoko Ohta, and Jun'ichi Tsujii. 2008. Corpus annotation for mining biomedical events from literature. *BMC bioinformatics*, 9(1):1.

Natalia Konstantinova, Sheila C.M. de Sousa, Noa P. Cruz, Manuel J. Maña, Maite Taboada, and Ruslan Mitkov. 2012. A review corpus annotated for negation, speculation and their scope. In Nicoletta Calzolari, Khalid Choukri, Thierry Declerck,

Mehmet Uğur Doğan, Bente Maegaard, Joseph Mariani, Jan Odijk, and Stelios Piperidis, editors, *Proceedings of the Eighth International Conference on Language Resources and Evaluation (LREC-2012)*, pages 3190–3195, Istanbul, Turkey, May. European Language Resources Association (ELRA).

Egoitz Laparra, Itziar Aldabe, and German Rigau. 2015. From TimeLines to StoryLines: A preliminary proposal for evaluating narratives. In *Proceedings of the First Workshop on Computing News Storylines*, pages 50–55, Beijing, China, July. Association for Computational Linguistics.

Valentina Bartalesi Lenzi, Giovanni Moretti, and Rachele Sprugnoli. 2012. CAT: the CELCT Annotation Tool. In Nicoletta Calzolari, Khalid Choukri, Thierry Declerck, Mehmet Uğur Doğan, Bente Maegaard, Joseph Mariani, Jan Odijk, and Stelios Piperidis, editors, *Proceedings of the Eighth International Conference on Language Resources and Evaluation (LREC-2012)*, pages 333–338, Istanbul, Turkey, May. European Language Resources Association (ELRA).

M. Antònia Martí, M. Teresa Martín-Valdivia, Mariona Taulé, Salud María Jiménez-Zafra, Montserrat Nofre, and Laia Marsó. 2016. La negación en español: análisis y tipología de patrones de negación. *Procesamiento del Lenguaje Natural*, 57:41–48.

Anne-Lyse Minard, Alessandro Marchetti, and Manuela Speranza. 2014. Event Factuality in Italian: Annotation of News Stories from the Ita-TimeBank. In *Proceedings of CLiC-it 2014, First Italian Conference on Computational Linguistic*, pages 260–264.

Anne-Lyse Minard, Manuela Speranza, and Tommaso Caselli. 2016. The EVALITA 2016 Event Factuality Annotation Task (FactA). In Pierpaolo Basile, Franco Cutugno, Malvina Nissim, Viviana Patti, and Rachele Sprugnoli, editors, *Proceedings of the 5th Evaluation Campaign of Natural Language Processing and Speech Tools for Italian (EVALITA 2016)*. aAcademia University Press.

Roser Morante and Walter Daelemans. 2012. Conandoyle-neg: Annotation of negation cues and their scope in conan doyle stories. In Nicoletta Calzolari, Khalid Choukri, Thierry Declerck, Mehmet Uğur Doğan, Bente Maegaard, Joseph Mariani, Jan Odijk, and Stelios Piperidis, editors, *Proceedings of the Eighth International Conference on Language Resources and Evaluation (LREC-2012)*, pages 1563–1568, Istanbul, Turkey, May. European Language Resources Association (ELRA).

Roser Morante, Sarah Schrauwen, and Walter Daelemans. 2011. Annotation of negation cues and their scope: Guidelines v1. *Computational linguistics and psycholinguistics technical report series, CTRS-003*.

Martha Palmer, Daniel Gildea, and Paul Kingsbury. 2005. The proposition bank: An annotated corpus of semantic roles. *Computational linguistics*, 31(1):71–106.

Sampo Pyysalo, Filip Ginter, Juho Heimonen, Jari Björne, Jorma Boberg, Jouni Järvinen, and Tapio Salakoski. 2007. BioInfer: a corpus for information extraction in the biomedical domain. *BMC Bioinformatics*, 8(1):50.

Kira Radinsky and Eric Horvitz. 2013. Mining the web to predict future events. In *Proceedings of the sixth ACM international conference on Web search and data mining*, pages 255–264. ACM.

Luca Serianni and Alberto Castelvecchi. 1988. *Grammatica italiana: italiano comune e lingua letteraria, suoni, forme, costrutti*. Utet.

Vanesa Stricker, Ignacio Iacobacci, and Viviana Cotik. 2015. Negated findings detection in radiology reports in spanish: an adaptation of negex to spanish. In *Workshop on Replicability and Reproducibility in Natural Language Processing: adaptive methods, resources and software at IJCAI 2015*.

Veronika Vincze, György Szarvas, Richárd Farkas, György Móra, and János Csirik. 2008. The bio-Scope corpus: biomedical texts annotated for uncertainty, negation and their scopes. *BMC bioinformatics*, 9(11):1.

Annotation of negation in the IULA Spanish Clinical Record Corpus

Montserrat Marimon, Jorge Vivaldi, Núria Bel
Universitat Pompeu Fabra
Roc Boronat 138
08018 Barcelona
{montserrat.marimon|jorge.vivaldi|nuria.bel}@upf.edu

Abstract

This paper presents the IULA Spanish Clinical Record Corpus, a corpus of 3,194 sentences extracted from anonymized clinical records and manually annotated with negation markers and their scope. The corpus was conceived as a resource to support clinical text-mining systems, but it is also a useful resource for other Natural Language Processing systems handling clinical texts: automatic encoding of clinical records, diagnosis support, term extraction, among others, as well as for the study of clinical texts. The corpus is publicly available with a CC-BY-SA 3.0 license.

1 Introduction

With the deployment of Electronic Health Records (EHR), much effort is being devoted to the development of text-mining tools that assist in converting information described in texts into structured data for applications that range from assisting in medical diagnosis to the coding of clinical findings and procedures to bill insurance companies. The ultimate objective of these tools is the extraction of factual knowledge from textual data. Therefore, they are mainly interested in developing special components that identify those facts that do not hold true, as in *patient without nodules*. The availability of annotated texts makes the use of supervised machine learning methods possible, and it also allows for a fair comparison and evaluation of different methods, thus contributing to the improvement of the technology.

In what follows, we describe the IULA Spanish Clinical Record Corpus (IULA-SCRC), a corpus of 3,194 sentences extracted from anonymized clinical records and manually annotated with negation markers and their scope, and the corresponding annotation guidelines.[1] To the best of our knowledge, this is the first corpus of medical Spanish texts manually annotated for negation, although two test-sets of about 500 and 1000 sentences for evaluating particular negation detection systems already exist, as described later in the Related Work section.

Because no standard negation annotation schema still exists, our annotation schema has taken into account the currently existing English corpora annotated for negation, trying to be comprehensive with current practices (Mutalik et al., 2001; Szarvas et al., 2008; Morante and Daelemans, 2012).

After this introductory section, in Section 2 we briefly describe negation structures in Spanish, in Section 3 we describe the corpus design, in Section 4 we present the guidelines we have followed to identify and classify negation information and in Section 5 we provide details of tags and statistics of the resulting annotated corpus, then, in Section 6 we review existing related corpora on which we have designed our annotation schema and, finally, in Section 7 we conclude.

2 Negation in Spanish

The most prominent negation marker in sentential negation in Spanish is the pre-verbal adverb *no* (1).

(1) *Juan **no** come carne.*   (Juan does not eat meat.)

Scope is the part of the sentence that is affected by a preceding negation marker that syntactically dominates it. Most frequently, sentential negation is expressed with a negation marker that scopes

---

[1] The corpus described in this paper has been made publicly available for research purposes and it is freely downloadable from: http://eines.iula.upf.edu/brat/\#/NegationOnCR_IULA

Proceedings of the Workshop Computational Semantics Beyond Events and Roles (SemBEaR), pages 43–52,
Valencia, Spain, April 4, 2017. ©2017 Association for Computational Linguistics

over the verb phrase. However, scope may also correspond to non-verbal phrases, as in (2), where the negation marker scopes over the adverb *siempre*.

(2) *Juan **no** siempre come carne.* (Juan does not always eat meat.)

In addition to the adverb *no*, there is a fairly heterogeneous group of pre-verbal words which also express sentential negation (3). These negation markers are: the pronouns *nada* (nothing) and *nadie* (nobody); the determinant *ninguno* (none); the adverbs *nunca*, *jamás* (never), *tampoco* (neither) and *nada* (nothing); and the phrases introduced by the coordination particle *ni* (nor).

(3) ***Nadie** ha venido.* (Nobody has come.)

Examples in (4) show a second pattern where these negation words follow the verb. In this position, they require a negation preceding the verb.

(4) (a) ***No** ha venido **nadie**.*   (Nobody has come.)

    (b) **Ha venido **nadie**.* (Has come nobody.)

In this structure we distinguish two groups of elements: a negative inducer and a negative polarity item. The first one allows the presence of the second one in post-verbal position.

Negative polarity items (NPIs) include: post-verbal negation words, indefinite NPs (5.a), and aspectual and scalar NPIs (5.b). Negative inducers (NIs) include: rhetorical interrogatives; comparative and superlative constructions (5.c); adverbial and nominal quantifiers (5.d); negative adverbs; negative verbs, nouns, and adjectives expressing doubt, opposition, deprivation or absence, or emotive factives (5.e); the conjunction *ni* (neiter); and the preposition *sin* (without).

(5) (a) *Juan **apenas** lee libro **alguno**.*   (Juan hardly reads any books.)

    (b) *Esto **no** vale **ni un pimiento**.* (This is not worth a light.)

    (c) *Juan es **más listo** que **nadie**.* (Juan is smarter than anyone.)

    (d) *Este examen es **demasido** difícil **para** que lo apruebe **nadie**.* (This test is too difficult for anyone to approve.)

    (e) *Es **improbable** que haya estado **nunca** en mi casa.* (It's unlikely she/he's ever been in my house.)

In addition to sentences and phrases, in Spanish single words can also be denied with the adverb *no* and by prefixation. In word negation, prefixes that express absence, opposition, falsehood, reversal, deprivation or removal, such as *a-*, *anti-* and *des-*, as in *amoral* (amoral), *anticapitalista* (anti-capitalist), and *desleal* (disloyal) are used. Other negative prefixes in Spanish are: *in-*, *sin-*, and *contra-*.

Finally, coordination and enumeration of negated words or phrases is also possible. In these structures, the first element follows the rules we have just presented, and the following coordinated elements can be preceded or not by the conjunction *ni*, but the last element must include the negative conjunction.

3   Corpus description

The basic material for compiling this resource was obtained from a set of 300 clinical reports from several services of one of the main hospitals in Barcelona (Spain). These reports were delivered to us already anonymized. After a first examination of these reports, it was observed that there was a set of 17 sections (e.g. "Physical Examination", "Diagnostic", "Procedures", "Reasons for consultation",...) that appeared in most of these reports. To compile the corpus only the five sections with more data were considered. In Table 1 we show the final number of sentences chosen from each section. Up to 3,000 sentences from these sections were separately collected and shuffled in order to make sure that no traceability of personal data was possible.

It is normal practice for automatic processing of clinical records to work with correct texts (Lai et al., 2015), thus, a simple set of regular expressions was used to correct most common misspellings. Remaining misspellings were manually corrected. Before annotating these reports, they were pre-processed for sentence identification.

Section	Sent.	%	Chosen
Physical exploration	5,193	34.61	1,090
Evolution	5,463	36.41	1,147
Radiology	1,751	11.67	367
Current process	980	6.53	205
Comp. explorations	1,619	10.79	339

Table 1: Statistics about corpus composition.

4 Annotation guidelines

In this section, we first introduce the underlying general annotation criteria. Second, we describe the guidelines we have followed to identify negation cues and their scopes.[2] Finally, we present the different classes of medical terms we have identified.

4.1 Underlying criteria

Our approach for annotating negation aims at supporting automatic processing for information extraction, which is usually supported by a dictionary coming either from a medical database or from a Named Entities recognition system. Information extraction systems are usually designed for extracting relations among entities. Ultimately, they are used to extract "facts". The presence of a negation marker might change the status of what a fact is.

Accordingly, in our annotation, first, negation markers are lexically defined: they are a list of words that change the factual status of what follows them, i.e. the scope. Second, we encode negation scope on syntactic terms: it is the maximal syntactic unit that is affected by the negation marker. However, as we will describe below, there are linguistic phenomena that escape from these general statements.

We annotate as negation markers only those negation words that affect the assertion made by other words in the sentence, because they change its factual status. This is the case, for instance, of the adverb *no* and some negative predicates, such as *ausencia de* (absence of).

However, we do not consider as negation markers those predicates that bear more information than bare negation. We discard verbs like *desaparecer* (to disappear), which indeed contains the information of a change of state. Other examples of predicates which are not considered negation markers are the verbs *retirar, suspenderse,* and *erradicar* (to remove, to call off, and to eradicate), and the noun *retirada* (removal). Also note that we do not consider the verb *negar* (to deny), as in *el paciente niega síntomas de abstinencia* (the patient denies withdrawal symptoms), a negation cue either, since, following clinician expert's advice,

this communication verb is considered, in factual terms, an statement of what someone says.

As for terms like *asintomático* (asymptomatic), which shows morphological prefixation (*a-, des-, dis-*), we decided to follow the current practice in medical text annotation for automatic processing (see Table 5) and not to annotate them as negation markers. Besides the fact that it is normal practice, we have considered the following motivations.[3] First, negative prefixed terms in Spanish medical domain are mostly lexicalized and most of them can easily be found in existing medical term databases. Second, most of them, in particular nouns, are coined terms, as they have a different specialized meaning from that of the non-prefixed counterpart and a different meaning, too, from the bare negation of the positive term, for instance *deshitratación* (dehydration) and *no hitratación* (no hydration) or *degeneración* (degeneration) vs. *no generación* (no generation). Third, not all prefixed words can be compositionally analyzed, as the non-prefixed counterpart does not exist (Dzuganova, 2006), *a-febril* (afebrile) vs. *a-morfo* (amorphous) or *ex-cluir* (exclude), for instance. Finally, prefixed words, as full words, can be in the scope of another negation marker. The interpretation of a double negation in these cases is uncertain, consider, for instance, *non-atypical hyperplasia* or *no mitral valve insufficiency*.

4.2 Negation cues

In our corpus, negation cues are words that express negation: adverbs, negative predicates, and the preposition *sin*. Examples in (6) show negations expressed by the preposition.

(6) (a) ***Sin** soplos audibles* (Without audible X); ***sin** signos de TVP* (without signs of X).

    (b) ***Sin** que se observen claros defectos de ventilación* (With no clear X observed).

The most frequent negative adverb in the corpus is the adverb *no*. This adverb negates verbal forms (7.a), nouns (7.b), and adjectives (7.c).

(7) (a) ***No** ausculto soplos* (I don't auscultate X); ***no** se palpan masas* (X are not palpated).

    (b) ***No** edemas en extremidades inferiores* (No X in lower extremities).

---

[2] In the examples we provide, cues are marked in bold and their scopes are underlined; in the next section, we present the actual tags we have used in the corpus. Also note that in the translated examples, medical terms are not translated, but they are replaced by "X".

[3] Note that in Spanish there are no negative suffixes like the English *less*.

(c) *Temblor discal* **no** *continuo en mano izquierda* (No continuous X in left hand).

Another negative adverb that we find in the corpus is *tampoco*. This adverb only negates verbal forms, as in (8).

(8) **Tampoco** *objetiva focos sépticos* (Neither objectify X).

We also mark as negation cues the following predicates: the verb *descartar* (to rule out) (9.a), the noun *ausencia de* (absence of) (9.b),[4] and the adjective *incapaz de* (unable to) (9.c).

(9) (a) *Se* **descarta** *enolismo* (X is ruled out).

   (b) **Ausencia de** *edemas* (Absence of X).

   (c) **Incapaz de** *levantarse de la silla* (Unable to get up from the chair).

The adjective *negativo* (negative), which is very frequent in medical texts, expresses negation in different ways. It may deny a sign, indicating on physical examination that a finding is not present (10.a); or it may deny a laboratory test, indicating that a substance or a reaction is not present (10.b). Sometimes, even though it clearly expresses negation, the specific bacteria or organism the cultures are negative for is not explicitly said in the sentence (10.c). We even have some examples where the negated test or sign is not expressed in the sentence: *negativo* is neither followed nor preceded by the noun it modifies. Thus, the adjective *negativo* is always marked as cue, even when its scope is not present in the sentence.

(10) (a) *Murphy* **negativo** (X negative).

   (b) *Serologías VHB y VHC* **negativos** (X negative).

   (c) *Hemocultivos de control* **negativos** (X negative).

Negative polarity items (11) (cf. Section 2) are also annotated as such. Note that the most frequent case is coordination.

(11) (a) *No objetivando* **ninguna** *focalidad neurológica mayor inmediata* (Not objectifying any inmediate main X).

---

[4] Note that the cue in (9.b) includes both the noun and the preposition, and that the cue in (9.c) includes the adjective and the preposition.

(b) **No** *masas* **ni** *megalias* (Neither X or Y); **sin** *soplos* **ni** *roces* (without X or Y).

Double negation sentences (12.a), in which two negatives yield affirmative, are not marked. Note that example (12.b) is not a false negative, since *desaparecer* (to disappear) is not considered a negation marker.

(12) (a) **No** *se puede* **descartar** *la etiología epiléptica de los episodios* (X can not be ruled out).

   (b) **Sin** *llegar a desaparecer del todo* (Without disappearing altogether).

4.3 Scope

Traditionally, scope is the part of the sentence that is being negated. The scope is determined on the basis of syntax: the maximal syntactic phrase that is affected by the marker. In our corpus, the negation cue is not included in its own scope.

As we show in (14), the scope of negated nouns extends to their complements and/or modifiers that follow them (14.a); the scope of negated adjectives extends to their complements, but the modified noun that in Spanish precedes the adjective is not annotated as scope (14.b); and the scope of negated verbs includes every verb dependent that follows it, and, we show in (14.c), constituents that precede the verb are not annotated as scope. This decision affects, in particular, verb subjects, which are however annotated in the scope when they are located after the verb (as in Bioscope). The only exception to this rule is when there is an unaccusative verb, for which we also annotate the subject, as we will see in example (19.d) below.

(14) (a) **No** <u>*edemas en extremidades inferiores*</u> (No X in lower extremities).

   (b) *Temblor discal* **no** <u>*continuo*</u> *en mano izquierda* (No continuous X in left hand).

   (c) <u>*El estudio realizado de forma ambulatoria hasta el momento*</u> **no** <u>*mostró alteraciones significativas*</u> (The study performed on an outpatient basis so far showed no significant alterations).

The preposition *sin* has a scope over the following noun phrase (15.a) and verb phrase (15.b) and, as before, all modifiers and complements of the nominal and verbal heads are included.

(15) (a) **Sin** *signos de TVP* (Without signs of X);
sin *contraindicaciones para el procedi-*
miento (Without contraindications to the
procedure).

(b) **Sin** *objetivar trombosis* (Without objectifying X), **sin** *que se observen claros*
defectos de ventilación (With no clear X
observed).

Negative predicate cues scope over their complements (16).

(16) (a) *Se* **descarta** *enolismo* (X is ruled out).

(b) **Ausencia de** *edemas* (Absence of X))

(c) **Incapaz de** *levantarse de la silla* (Unable to get up from the chair).

Because of its special characteristics already
explained in section 4.2, the adjective *negativo*
scopes over its modified noun, which precedes it
(17.a) or over the PP that includes the denied test
or sign (17.b). When this adjective functions as an
attribute or a predicative complement (17.c), the
scope is the subject. Finally, when the subject is a
relative pronoun, we annotate as the scope its antecedent (17.d).

(17) (a) *Focalidad* **negativa** (X negative).

(b) **Negativo** *para FOP* (Negative for X).

(c) *Las serologías para VIH, VHB y VHC*
resultaron **negativas** (X were negative).
El urocultivo es **negativo** (X is negative).

(d) *Se tomó* *urocultivo, que resultó* **negativo**
(It was taken X, which was negative).

In coordination, the cue scopes over all coordinated elements (18).

(18) (a) **No** *masas* **ni** *megalias* (Neither X nor
Y).

(b) **Sin** *soplos* **ni** *roces* (Without X or Y).

(c) **No** *refiere síndrome miccional, cambios*
en el ritmo deposicional **ni** *otra sinto-*
matología acompanante (Does nor refer
X, or Y, or Z).

Discontinuous scopes are also annotated. These
are examples like (19.a), where the adjective appears between the noun and its modifier, ellipti-
cal constructions, such as (19.b), relative clauses,
where the antecedent of the relative pronoun is
also annotated as discontinuous scope (19.c), and

unaccusative verbs, whose subject is also included
in the scope of the negation cue, even though it
precedes the verb (19.d).

(19) (a) *Hemocultivos* **negativos** *de control*
(Control negative X).

(b) *Parcialmente* *orientado* *(sí en tiempo y*
persona, **no** *en espacio)* (Partially ori-
ented (yes in time and person, not in
space)).

(c) *Se trató con* *antibiótico que* **no** *recuerda*
(S/he was treated with antibiotics which
s/he does not remember).

(d) *El dolor* **no** *mejorado con nolotil* (Pain
has not improved with nolotil).

4.4 Medical term classes

Most of the cues that are present in the corpus
scope over medical named entities. Table 2 shows
the classes we have distinguished among these entities. In the next section we will present the actual
tags we have used for manually annotating them in
the corpus.

Class	Used for
Body structure	- Anatomical structure - Body part - Organ or organ component - Deformity - Tissue, ...
Substance & Pharmacological/ biological product	- Pharmacological substance - Biological substance - Enzyme - Body substance - Diagnostic substance, ...
Clinical finding	- Disease or syndrome - Finding - Sign/Symptom - Abnormality - Clinical state, ...
Procedure	- Diagnostic procedure - Laboratory procedure - Therapeutic Procedure - Administration of medicine - Health care activity, ...

Table 2: Medical term classes.

This classification was taken from the
SNOMED Clinical Terms (SNOMED CT), a
multilingual clinical healthcare terminology

used in clinical documentation.[5] This resource defines 19 top level hierarchies (or classes), we have chosen five of them which are the most frequent classes found in this type of reports. For operative reasons we collapse SNOMED classes "Substance" and "Pharmacological/biological product" in a single medical term class.

5   Corpus Annotation

The annotation was made with Brat, a web-based tool for text annotation.[6]   In this section, we present the actual tags we have used in the annotation. We also discuss the annotation agreement and provide some statistics of the corpus.

5.1   Tags

In Table 3 we show the list of tags that are used to mark negation cues and the text spans that function as scope. In addition, tagged links are used to describe the relationships between them: we use the tag `Scope` to link scopes to negation cues (Figure 1 and Figure 2) and the tag `DiscScope` to annotate discontinuous scope phenomena explicitly (Figure 3).

Tag	Entity
Negmarker	*no, tampoco, sin*
NegPredMarker	negative verbs, nouns and adjectives
NegPolItem	*ni, ninguno,...*
BODY	body structure
SUBS	substance...
DISO	clinical finding
PROC	procedure
Phrase	nonmedical text spans

Table 3: Tags for entities.

Negation cues are marked by two different tags. We use the tag `NegMarker` for basic negation markers (Figure 1.a-c): the adverbs *no* and *tampoco*, and the preposition *sin*. We use the tag `NegPredMarker` for negative verbs, nouns, and adjectives (Figure 1.d-f).   In addition, the tag `NegPolItem` (Figure 1.b-c) is used for NPIs.

We have used four tags for the medical named entities (see Section 4.4) that are in the scope of a negation marker: `BODY` for body structures, `SUBS` for substances and pharmacologi-

[5]http://www.ihtsdo.org/
[6]http://brat.nlplab.org/

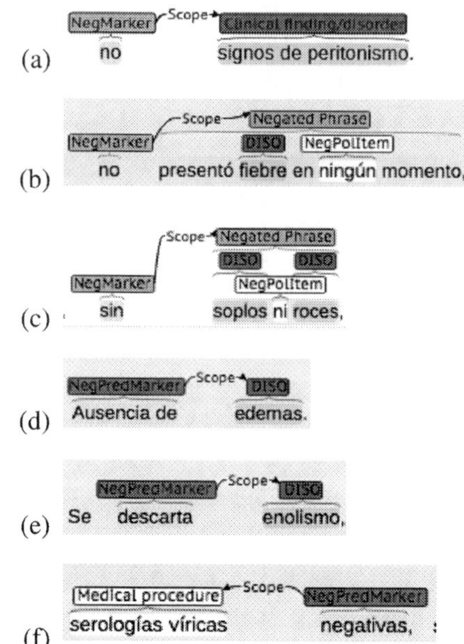

Figure 1: Annotation examples: tags for negation cues.

cal/biological products, `DISO` for clinical findings (Figure 1.c-e), and `PROC` for medical procedures (Figure 1.b). In addition, we use the tag `Phrase` for:

- Negated phrases that are not of the medical domain (Figure 2.a).

- Text spans that are not headed by an entity belonging to one of the medical classes we have considered (Figure 2.b).

- Complete coordinated phrases (Figure 2.c-e).

5.2   Agreement analysis

In order to evaluate the guidelines, 500 sentences were annotated by three computational linguists advised by a clinician. Disagreements were discussed after three different annotation rounds until reaching a consensus. Annotation guidelines were updated accordingly. Then, we measured the consistency of the annotations for the negation markers and their scope, but not of the entities annotations which were validated using SNOMED. The inter-annotator agreement Kappa rates were 0.85 between annotators 1 and 2, and 1 and 3; 0.88 between annotators 2 and 3.

Figure 2: Annotation examples: tags for scope entities.

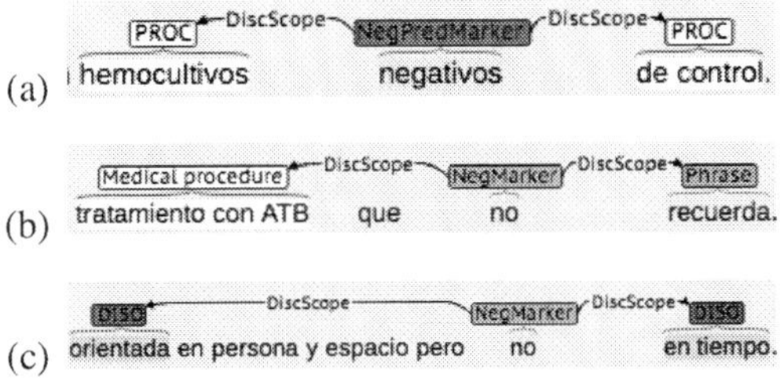

Figure 3: Annotation examples: discontinuous scopes.

5.3 Corpus statistics

Final annotated corpus details are in Table 4. The most frequent tag for cues is Negmarker, which appears 1,007 times (519 marking the adverb *no* and 488 marking the preposition *sin*). The most frequent NPI is *ni*, which appears 109 times, whereas the most frequent negative predicate is *negativo*, which appears 63 times.

6 Related work

Most of existing corpora in the biomedical domain annotated with negation have been developed as test sets of systems to detect negated expressions. Most of these resources show a common set of annotations (see Table 5). All annotate negation markers and their scope. Negative predicates are

Number of sentences	3,194
Number of annotated sentences	1,093
Number of Negmarker entities	1,007
Number of NegPredMarker entities	86
Number of NegPolItem entities	114
Number of BODY entities	7
Number of SUBS entities	14
Number of DISO entities	1,064
Number of PROC entities	93
Number of Phrase entities	278

Table 4: Corpus statistics.

annotated by most of them, but each one considers a different list of predicates. None annotates morphological-related negation phenomena (prefixes or suffixes). In general, discontinuous scope is not taken into account. Finally, no one annotates the actual negation marker within the scope. Now, we briefly describe the most salient characteristics of each system and resulting annotation.

Negfinder by (Mutalik et al., 2001) uses a lexical scanner with regular expressions to identify negation and a context-free grammar parser to associate negation markers to their scope. In the test-set only bare negative words are annotated, while words (medical terms) whose meaning is change of state, e.g. *stopping* or *discontinuing a drug*, are not annotated, nor are medical terms having a negative prefix (*akinesia*).

Chapman et al. (2001) developed NegEx, a simple regular expression-based algorithm to determine whether a finding or disease mentioned within medical reports was present or absent. NegEx implements (up to 35) negative and pseudo-negative phrases, limits their scope and rules out sentences having double negation. There are different versions of NegEx (South et al., 2007; Harkema et al., 2009), and it has been adapted to Swedish (Skeppstedt, 2011), French (Deléger and Grouin, 2012), Dutch (Afzal et al., 2014), and Spanish (Costumero et al., 2014). In addition, the systems developed by Sohn et al. (2012) (DepNeg) and Mehrabi et al. (2015) (DEEPEN) are based on or use NegEx complemented with a dependency-based parser to improve scope detection. And, in another line of research, Goldin and Chapman (2003) use Naive Bayes and Decision Trees to increase the NegEx's precision of negation with only the word "not". In these NegEx-based systems, negative predicates such as *denies,*

Corpus/System	Language	Technique	Uncertainty	Basic Negation	Morph. Neg.	Negative Pred.	Disc. Scope	Focus
Negfinder	EN	lexical scanner + CFG	no	yes	no	yes	no	no
NegEx	EN,ES GE,SW	Regular Expression pattern matching	no	yes	no	yes	no	no
DepNeg & DEEPEN	EN	dependency parsing	no	yes	no	yes	no	no
Goldin & Chapman's	EN	machine learning NB & DT	no	yes	no	no	no	no
Cotik et al.'s	ES	rules PoS-tag NegEx & ST	no	yes	no	yes	no	no
NegHunter	EN	rules based on grammatical info	no	yes	no	yes	no	no
Elkin et al.'s	EN	negation ontology	yes	yes	no	yes	no	no
BioScope	EN	manual	yes	yes	no	yes	no	no
BioInfer	EN	manual	no	yes	no	no	no	no
IULA-SCRC	ES	manual	no	yes	no	yes	yes	no

Table 5: Comparison of different proposals to negation annotation in the biomedical domain.

declines and *no complaints of* are annotated.

Cotik et al. (2016) developed syntactic techniques based in rules derived from PoS tagging patterns, constituent tree patterns and dependency tree patterns, and an adaptation of NegEx, to determine if a medical term is under the scope of negation in radiology reports written in Spanish. Since they translate the Negative predicates provided by the NEgEx tool, these are included in the test-set.

Another rule-based negation algorithm is NegHunter, developed by Gindl et al. (2008), which uses grammatic information such as tense and part-of-speech to detect negation in clinical practice guidelines lexically marked by adverbs, prepositions and a few predicates (*absence, freedom, deny, decline* and *lack*).

Finally, Elkin et al. (2005) developed a mechanism for automated annotation of negation of clinical concepts invoking an ontology. Negative predicates are annotated, including the verb *to deny*.

As for other annotated biomedical corpora, the following resources have been developed with explicit aim of somehow annotating negation. In general, they annotate more cases of negation than the test-sets just reviewed. In what follows we review their most salient characteristics.[7]

The BioScope corpus (Szarvas et al., 2008) gathers medical and biological texts (20,879 sentences) annotated for negation cues, speculation and their linguistic scope. The minimal unit that expresses negation is marked as cue and its scope is extended to the largest syntactic phrase. The scope includes the negation cue, and leaves the subject out, but only in active sentences.

The BioInfer corpus (Pyysalo et al., 2007) contains 1,100 sentences from abstracts of research articles where biomedical relations are annotated for negation.

The 2010 i2b2/VA NLP Challenge Corpus (information extracted from (Wu et al., 2014)) contains 871 de-identified reports from different hospitals and medical centers. Negation as such is not annotated, but each medical term is associated with different tags, one of these being "absent" which seems to match with what others consider negated expressions. This annotation includes also what we have called morphology-related and inherently negated terms such as *afebrile*.

Finally, the BioNLP Genia Event Extraction Corpus (Kim et al., 2008) is frequently mentioned

---

[7]Some of these corpus are only found in the literature and are not publicly available.

in the related literature. However, although a negation attribute is mentioned at event level, cues and
their scope are not annotated.

7 Conclusions

In this article, we have introduced the annotation
guidelines of the IULA Spanish Clinical Record
Corpus annotated for negation. We have described the underlying criteria and we have motivated the choice of a syntactically-based general
criterion, as well as the relation of our annotation
schema with other negation-annotated corpora already available, although all but one are for English. The corpus currently contains about 3000
sentences and it is licensed with Creative Com-
mons 3.0 CC-BY-SA license. This resource has
been developed for supporting text-mining systems either to serve as a test set for rule based
systems or as training data for machine learning
based systems. Nevertheless, it is also a good resource for the study of clinical texts.

Acknowledgments

We want to acknowledge the support of Dra. Pi-
lar Bel-Rafecas, clinician, and the comments and
suggestions of the two anonymous reviewers that
have contributed to improve the final version of
this paper. This work was partially supported
by the project TUNER (TIN2015-65308-C5-1-R,
MINECO/FEDER)

References

Zubair Afzal, Ewoud Pons, Ning Kang, Miriam
Sturkenboom, Martijn Schuemie, and Jan Kors.
2014. ContextD: an algorithm to identify contextual properties of medical terms in a Dutch clinical
corpus. *BMC Bioinformatics*, 15(373):1–12.

Wendy W. Chapman, Will Bridewell, Paul Hanbury,
Gregory F. Cooper, and Bruce G. Buchanan. 2001.
A simple algorithm for identifying negated findings
and diseases in discharge summaries. *Journal of
Biomedical Informatics*, 34(5):301–310.

Roberto Costumero, Federico López, Consuelo
Gonzalo-Martín, Marta Millan, and Ernestina
Menasalvas. 2014. An approach to detect negation
on medical documents in Spanish. In *Brain Infor-
matics and Health*, volume 8609, pages 366–375.
Springer International Publishing.

Viviana Cotik, Vanesa Stricker, Jorge Vivaldi, and Ho-
racio Rodríguez. 2016. Syntactic methods for negation detection in radiology reports in spanish. In
*Proceedings of the 15th Workshop on Biomedical
Natural Language Processing (BIONLP 16)*, pages
156–166. Association for Computational Linguistics, Berlin, Germany.

Louise Deléger and Cyril Grouin. 2012. Detecting negation of medical problems in French clinical notes. In *Proceedings of the 2nd ACM SIGHIT
International Health Informatics Symposium*, pages
697–702.

Bozena Dzuganova. 2006. *Bratislavske Lekarske
Listy*, 107(8):332–335.

Peter L. Elkin, Steven H. Brown, Brent A. Bauer,
Casey S. Husser, William Carruth, Larry R.
Bergstrom, and Dietlind L. Wahner-Roedler. 2005.
A controlled trial of automated classification of
negation from clinical notes. *BMC Medical Infor-
matics and Decision Making*, 5(13).

Stefan Gindl, Katharina Kaiser, and Silvia Miksch.
2008. Syntactical Negation Detection in Clinical
Practice Guidelines. *Studies in Health Technology
and Informatics*, 136:187–192.

Ilya M. Goldin and Wendy W. Chapman. 2003. Learning to detect negation with 'not' in medical texts. In
*Proceedings of the Workshop on Text Analysis and
Search for Bioinformatics at the 26th Annual International ACM SIGIR Conference (SIGIR-2003)*.

Henk Harkema, John N. Dowling, Tyler Thornblade,
and Wendy W. Chapman. 2009. Context: An algorithm for determining negation, experiencer, and
temporal status from clinical reports. *Journal of
Biomedical Informatics*, 42(5):839–851.

Jin-Dong Kim, Tomoko Ohta, and Jun'ichi Tsujii.
2008. Corpus annotation for mining biomedical
events from literature. *BMC Bioinformatics*, 9(10).

Kenneth H. Lai, Maxim Topaz, Foster R. Goss, and
Li Zhou. 2015. Automated misspelling detection
and correction in clinical free-text records. *Journal
of Biomedical Informatics*, 55(C):188–195.

Saeed Mehrabi, Anand Krishnan, Sunghwan Sohn,
Alexandra M. Roch, Heidi Schmidt, Joe Kesterson,
Chris Beesley, Paul R. Dexter, C. Max Schmidt,
Hongfang Liu, and Mathew J. Palakal. 2015.
DEEPEN: A negation detection system for clinical
text incorporating dependency relation into NegEx.
Journal of Biomedical Informatics, 54:213–219.

Roser Morante and Walter Daelemans. 2012. Conan
doyleneg: Annotation of negation in conan doyle
stories. In *Proceedings of the Eighth International
Conference on Language Resources and Evaluation
(LREC-2012)*, pages 1563–1568, Istanbul, Turkey.

Pradeep G. Mutalik, Aniruddha Deshpande, and
Prakash M. Nadkarni. 2001. Use of General-
purpose Negation Detection to Augment Concept
Indexing of Medical Documents: A Quantitative
Study Using the UMLS. *Journal of the American
Medical Informatics Association*, 8(6):598–609.

Sampo Pyysalo, Filip Ginter, Juho Heimonen, Jari Bjorne, Jorma Boberg, Jouni Jarvinen, and Tapio Salakoski. 2007. Bioinfer: a corpus for information extraction in the biomedical domain. *BMC Bioinformatics*, 8(50).

Maria Skeppstedt. 2011. Negation Detection in Swedish Clinical Text: An Adaption of NegEx to Swedish. *Journal of Biomedical Semantics*, 2(3):1–12.

Sunghwan Sohn, Stephen Wu, and Christopher G. Chute. 2012. Dependency parser-based negation detection in clinical narratives. In *AMIA Summits on Translational Science Proceedings*, pages 1–8.

Brett R. South, Shobha Phansalkar, Ashwin Deepak Swaminathan, Sylvain Delisle, Trish Perl, and Matthew H. Samore. 2007. Adaptation of the NegEx algorithm to Veterans Affairs electronic text notes for detection of influenza-like illness (ILI). In *AMIA Symposium*, pages 11–18. American Medical Informatics Association.

György Szarvas, Veronika Vincze, Richárd Farkas, and János Csirik. 2008. The BioScope Corpus: Annotation for Negation, Uncertainty and Their Scope in Biomedical Texts. In *Proceedings of the Workshop on Current Trends in Biomedical Natural Language Processing*, pages 38–45, Stroudsburg, PA, USA.

Stephen Wu, Timothy Miller, James Masanz, Matt Coarr, Scott Halgrim, and David Carrell. 2014. Negation's Not Solved: Generalizability Versus Optimizability in Clinical Natural Language Processing. *PLoS ONE*, 9(11).

Annotating Negation in Spanish Clinical Texts

Noa P. Cruz Díaz[1], Roser Morante Vallejo[2], Manuel J. Maña López[3], Jacinto Mata Vázquez[3] and
Carlos L. Parra Calderón[1]

[1]IBiS/Virgen del Rocío University Hospital/CSIC/University of Seville
[2]CLTL Lab, VU Amsterdam
[3]Departamento de Tecnologías de la Información, University of Huelva
{noapatricia.cruz.exts,carlos.parra.sspa}@juntadeandalucia.es
{r.morantevallejo}@vu.nl
{manuel.mana,jacinto.mata}@dti.uhu.es

Abstract

In this paper we present on-going work on annotating negation in Spanish clinical documents. A corpus of anamnesis and radiology reports has been annotated by two domain expert annotators with negation markers and negated events. The Dice coefficient for inter-annotator agreement is higher than 0.94 for negation markers and higher than 0.72 for negated events. The corpus will be publicly released when the annotation process is finished, constituting the first corpus annotated with negation for Spanish clinical reports available for the NLP community.

1 Introduction

In this paper we present the UHU-HUVR corpus of Spanish clinical reports annotated with negation information. Negation processing (Morante and Blanco, 2012) is an emergent task in Natural Language Processing (NLP). Initially, negation processing systems were developed to detect negation in clinical texts in order to extract accurate information about the patients. The systems were rule-based (Chapman et al., 2001) because of the lack of annotated corpora to train machine learning systems. Currently, annotated corpora are still scarce due to the legal and ethical requirements that have to be fulfilled. In addition, most of the corpora only contain documents written in English. An example is the BioScope corpus (Szarvas et al., 2008) which contains 1,954 radiology reports from the Computational Medicine Center in Cincinnati, annotated for negations and uncertainty along with the scopes of each phenomenon.

For Spanish clinical reports, to the best of our knowledge, there are only a few attempts to anno-tate negation, mostly as a secondary task within broader projects, and none of the annotated resources are publicly available. For example, Costumero et al. (2014) adapted the NegEx algorithm (Chapman et al., 2001) to detect negated clinical conditions in Spanish written medical documents. Although the authors mention that 500 medical texts have been manually annotated, they do not provide more information about this gold-standard. Oronoz et al. (2015), annotated negated adverse drug reactions, but they did not annotate the words expressing negation. The negation was annotated as a modifier of the disorder or drug. Stricker et al. (2015) used a dataset composed of about 85,600 reports of ultrasonography studies performed in a Spanish public hospital. Clinical findings were annotated in a subset of the reports as being affirmed (if it was possible to infer that the finding was present in the patient) or negated (if the finding was absent). The annotations were recently expanded by Cotik et al. (2016), including the values *probable* (if it was not certain that the finding was present, but it was probable) and *doubt* (if the finding corresponded to the past or if it was not clear for the annotator if the finding was present or not). None of the studies provides information about the availability of the corpora.

Being aware of the limitations of the current approaches and the necessity of filling this gap, we present the first version of the UHU-HUVR Corpus, a set of clinical documents annotated with negation markers and their linguistic scope. The annotated corpus and its guidelines will be made publicly available. The paper is structured as follows: Section 2 describes the annotation process and provides information about the corpus. Section 3 presents the results of the agreement analysis and discusses difficult or interesting cases. Finally, conclusions and future work are presented in Section 4.

Proceedings of the Workshop Computational Semantics Beyond Events and Roles (SemBEaR), pages 53–58,
Valencia, Spain, April 4, 2017. ©2017 Association for Computational Linguistics

2 Annotating Negation in Spanish Clinical Reports

The corpus that we present consists of 604 clinical reports from the Virgen del Rocío Hospital in Seville (Spain). Specifically, the set of documents consists of diagnosis information of 276 radiology reports and the personal history of 328 anamnesis reports written in free text, as shown in Table 1. The reports were randomly collected among reports from the first semester of 2013, and were fully anonymized in order to satisfy legal and ethical issues. The radiology documents are longer than the anamnesis documents (339.05 and 157.66 average words per document respectively), but the average words per sentence is similar (17.50 versus 16.87).

	Anamnesis	Radiology
#Docs	328	276
#Sentences	3,065	5,347
#Words	51,712	93,579
Avg. length docs (sentences)	9.34	19.37
Avg. length docs (words)	157.66	339.05
Avg. length sentences (words)	16.87	17.50

Table 1: Statistics about the UHU-HUVR corpus.

The entire corpus was annotated by two domain experts who followed the guidelines that we developed. The annotation process started with two pilot experiments. In the first one, the authors annotated 7 reports in order to gain insight to produce the first version of the guidelines, which was written by one of the authors, who is a linguistics expert. In the second one 100 anamnesis documents were annotated by the two annotators in order to train them, and test and improve the guidelines. These documents are not included in the final corpus. During all the annotation process, the annotators were not allowed to communicate with each other. The problematic cases that they encountered were discussed with the expert linguist and author of the guidelines. As work in progress, another author who is expert annotator is currently solving the disagreement cases, acting as adjudicator, in order to generate the gold-standard corpus. The annotation tool used was CAT (Lenzi et al., 2012). Two markables were defined (negation marker and negated event) plus a negation relation between the marker and the event.

The annotation task consisted on annotating the events that are affected by contextual negation, as well as the words that express negation. We will refer to these words as *markers*. In the examples that follow, negated events are marked within brackets and negation markers in bold. In example 1, the word *no* is the negation marker and *alteraciones en el luminograma aéreo de tráquea* is the event affected by this negation. Examples of events with negative polarity are the following ones:[1]

1. **No** visualizamos [alteraciones en el luminograma aéreo de tráquea]. (En. We did not visualize alterations in the aerial luminogram of trachea.)

2. **No** [aumentos ganglionares hilio mediastínicos] **ni** [hallazgos de interés a lo largo del esófago]. (En. No mediastinal hilum nodal enlargement nor findings of interest along the esophagus.)

3. **Sin** [lesiones óseas focales que sugieran metástasis en este barrido]. (En. No focal bone lesions suggestive of metastasis in this scan.)

4. Desde hace 20 años **abandono** radical del [hábito tabáquico]. (En. During the last 20 years radical stopping of smoking habit.)

The annotation guidelines follow closely the Thyme corpus guidelines (Styler IV et al., 2014) with some adaptations. We defined as clinical event any event that is relevant to elaborate the clinical chronology of a patient such as a diagnosis, tumors, habits, medical tests, or events related to the functional evaluation of the patient. Events that do not contribute clinical information are not annotated. The difficulty of annotating events lies not just in identifying what is an event, but in determining which is the chain of words that express the event. We decided to annotate all the words that express the event, excluding punctuation marks. In Example (1) the full NP is annotated as event: *alteraciones en el luminograma aéreo de tráquea*. For negation markers, the minimum number of words is annotated.

We do not always annotate the mentions of negative results of a test as negation markers because the fact that a test is negative does not necessarily imply that a clinical event is not happening. In Example (5) no negation is annotated because, although the results of the Z-N stain are negative,

---

[1] We provide between parentheses English translations for all examples.

the test has taken place. However, when the name of the test is the same as the name of the clinical condition, such as a disease, then the negative results are annotated as negation because the negative result indicates that the patient does not have the disease (see Example (6)).

5. Técnicas de Z-N (normal y largo) negativo. (En. Negative Z-N stain (normal and long).)

6. Serología materna: [Toxoplasma]: **Negativo**. [VHB]: **Negativo**. [Rubeola]: **Negativo**. [Lues]: **Negativo**. (En. Maternal serology: Toxoplasma: Negative. VHB: Negative. Rubella: Negative. Lues: negative.)

In addition, negative results are sometimes expressed with the "-" sign, which was annotated as negation marker in the same cases as indicated above.

As for affixal negation, we take a pragmatic approach and annotate the full word where the affix occurs as a negation marker and as a negated event, when an event is negated. It is the case of *afebril* (En. without fever), where *a-* is the negation marker. Due to limitations of the tools we could not split the affixes in order to mark them independently.

Finally, some coordination structures involve negation markers. In this cases, each negation marker in the structure has its own scope, as shown in Example (7), where the first coordination marker *no* scopes over *alteraciones a nivel de los distintos ligamentos y estructuras músculo-tendinosas* and Example (8), where the second coordination marker *así como* scopes over *alteraciones ... de las restantes partes blandas*. In clinical reports, some expressions like *así como*, which are usually not negation markers, are used as such, and thus, we decided to mark them as negation markers, even if what brings negation to the event is the coordination structure and not only the second coordinating element. We have also marked "/" as negation marker when it acts as a coordinating particle, as in Examples (9) and (10).

7. **No** hemos observado [alteraciones a nivel de los distintos ligamentos y estructuras músculo-tendinosas], así como de las restantes partes blandas. (En. We have not observed alterations at the level of the different ligaments and musculo-tendinous structures, as well as of the other soft parts.)

8. No hemos observado [alteraciones] a nivel de los distintos ligamentos y estructuras músculo-tendinosas, **así como** [de las restantes partes blandas]. (En. We have not observed alterations at the level of the different ligaments and muscle-tendon structures, as well as of the other soft parts.)

9. Actualmente **no** hay evidencia de [nódulos pulmonares] / adenomegalias mediastínicas. (En. No evidence of pulmonary nodules / mediastinal adenomegalies)

10. Actualmente no hay evidencia de nódulos pulmonares / [adenomegalias mediastínicas].

2.1 Negation in Spanish Clinical Texts

The annotations show that negation is a frequent phenomenon in Spanish clinical texts. As it is shown in Table 2, more than 22% of the sentences in radiology reports contain negation markers, whereas in anamnesis reports this percentage is even higher, 35.20%. This fact is related to the nature of the two types of documents. Whereas a radiology report reflects the radiologists observations, the anamnesis report describes the history of the patient, including clinical conditions that the patient has not gone through.

In Spanish clinical domain, (Oronoz et al., 2015) reported that 27.58% of diseases presented in a corpus of electronic health records are negated. Although this percentage is not directly comparable with the percentage of negated sentences shown in Table 2, the numbers seem similar. The frequency of negation in Spanish for the reviews domain is sensibly higher. Martí et al. (2016) analysed the 75% of SFU Review SP-NEG corpus and claimed that 46.64% of sentences contain at least one negation. However, unpublished analysis about the entire SFU Review SP-NEG corpus shown that the amount of sentences that contain at least one negation in this corpus is the 31.90%, which represents a similar value to negation frequency in anamnesis reports.

	#Negation sentences	% Negation sentences	# Negation markers
Anamnesis	1,079	35.20	1,572
Radiology	1,219	22.80	1,985

Table 2: Negation statistics in the UHU-HUVR corpus.

Negation markers in the UHU-HUVR corpus amounted to 69 in the anamnesis subcollection and 32 in the radiology subcollection, with the top 10 most frequent markers shown in Tables 3 and 4. It is interesting to note that, in Spanish, the first two markers, *no* ('no') and *sin* ('without'), constitute more than 70% of the total frequency of all the markers found in the corpus, while the remaining markers cover only about 30%. 28 of the markers are common for radiology and anamnesis reports. It is also interesting to see that signs as "/" or "-" are considered to be negation markers. A specific negation marker of the radiology reports is *namc* which stands for *no alergias medicamentosas conocidas* (En. no known drug allergies).

Marker	Frequency	%	Acc. %
no	936	59.54	59.54
sin	197	12.53	72.07
ni	143	9.10	81.17
niega	66	4.20	85.37
namc	31	1.97	87.34
negativo	26	1.65	88.99
nunca	20	1.27	90.26
o	19	1.21	91.47
-	14	0.89	92.36
independiente	11	0.70	93.06

Table 3: The most frequent negation markers in the anamnesis subcollection of the UHU-HUVR corpus.

Marker	Frequency	%	Acc. %
sin	877	44.18	44.18
no	662	33.35	77.53
ni	258	13.00	90.53
así como	28	1.41	91.94
ausencia	27	1.36	93.30
o	27	1.36	94.66
tampoco	14	0.71	95.37
desaparecido	7	0.35	95.72
/	6	0.30	96.02
asimetría	6	0.30	96.32
inespecíficas	6	0.30	96.62
inespecífico	6	0.30	96.92

Table 4: The most frequent negation markers in the radiology subcollection of the UHU-HUVR corpus.

3 Preliminary results

Table 5 illustrates the results obtained for Inter-Annotator Agreement (IAA) between the two annotators in terms of Dice's coefficient measure (Dice, 1945) as calculated by the CAT annotation tool. We are currently working on the adjudication process. The IAA for markers is high and almost equal in radiology (0.949) and anamnesis (0.947) reports, whereas the IAA for events is lower than for markers. The IAA for events in radiology reports is lower (0.729) than for anamnesis reports (0.840).

	Marker Level		Token Level	
	Markers	Events	Markers	Events
Anamnesis	0.947	0.840	0.947	0.896
Radiology	0.949	0.729	0.949	0.860

Table 5: Preliminary Inter-Annotator Agreement in terms of Dice's coefficient.

The lower scores for radiology reports can be explained by the fact that the average length for events in anamnesis reports is lower (2,10 words) than in radiology reports (2,81 words), and thus there are more tokens that can be differently annotated for the same event. Additionally, it is also the case that interpreting the information in the radiology reports requires more specialised knowledge than interpreting the information in the anamnesis reports. In the latter, the events are better delimited and there are certain frequent negated expressions that are repeated throughout the reports, such as *No* or *Niega* followed by an event, as in the examples below.

11. **No** [hábitos tóxicos]. (En. No toxic habits.)

12. **Niega** [alergias]. (En. Denies allergies.)

13. **No** [alergias medicamentosas]. (En. No drug allergies.)

In the radiology reports it is more difficult to agree on which is the event affected by the marker, as in Example (14).

14. **Sin** [hallazgos en la distribución visualización de asas y mesos intestinales y órganos pélvicos]. (En. No findings in the distribution visualization of intestinal loops and mesenteries and pelvic organs.)

Furthermore, in many radiology reports incorrect syntactic constructions are used, as in Example (15), where two negation markers are used after each other forming an agrammatical expression *ni tampoco*, which can be confusing for the annotators.

15. **No** se [realza] **ni tampoco** [las ramas tributarias segmentarias de lngula] y [LII]. (En. It is not enhanced neither the segmental tributary branches of lingula and LII.)

The IAA is similar to the IAA reported for the clinical collection of the BioScope corpus (Szarvas et al., 2008) in English, where the IAA between the two annotators was 0.907 for the markers and 0.762 for the scope. This shows that the difficulty of the task is independent of the language in which the documents are written and inherent to the type of texts.

Disagreement cases were analysed by the adjudicator who decides on the correct annotations. Most of the disagreements were the result of a human error, i.e., the annotators missed a word or included a word that did not belong either to the event or to the marker. However, other cases of disagreement can be explained by the difficulty of the task and the lack of clear guidance.

A great number of disagreements are related to the difficulty of detecting what is an event and which is the chain of words that express the event, as in Example (16), where the first annotator identified as event the words *Contraste I* while the second one annotated *Contraste I . V .*, but none annotated the correct span of the event.

16. **Sin** [Contraste I. V. de Senos Paranasales] (En. Without Contrast I.V. of paranasal sinuses.)

Cases in which negation is expressed by affixes were a source of disagreement due to the lack of initial guidelines. An example is the word *afebril* which expresses absence of fever. In these cases, the whole word should be marked both as an event and as a marker. In contrast, words such as incontinencia urinaria ('urinary incontinence'), which contain a negation affix (*in-* in this case) do not have to be annotated as negation markers since the clinical condition that they express is not negated.

More cases of disagreement involve a false double negation as shown in Example (17). One of the annotators identified two markers (*no* and *tampoco*) instead of one, which is the correct solution because this is not a case of double negation.

17. Nunca le han dicho que tuviera anemia porque **no** [ha acudido tampoco al médico]. (En. (S)he has never been told that (s)he had anemia because (s)he did not go to the doctor either.)

Another source of disagreement are cases in which one marker negates several events, as in Example (18). One annotator annotated the word *niega* as a marker and marked as event the rest of the sentence, while the other annotator also identified the word *niega* as a marker but annotated each event separately, which is the correct solution. This case represents an enumeration where several events are negated by the same marker. Therefore, each event had to be annotated and related to the marker independently, generating 4 negation relations.

18. **Niega** [HTA], [diabetes], [dislipemias] u [otros FR vascular]. (En. Denies AHT, diabetes, dyslipidemia or other FR vascular.)

Jiménez-Zafra et al. (2016) encountered the same type of disagreements when annotating a Spanish review corpus (Taboada et al., 2006) with negation information, i.e., lack of agreement between annotators about the scope, the event and the discontinuities. This type of errors amount to 63.26% of the total. They also mentioned semantic problems that arose from the interpretation of negation patterns in comparative and contrastive constructions.

4 Conclusions

We have presented the first version of the UHU-HUVR Corpus, a collection of 604 clinical documents written in Spanish and annotated with negation markers, negated events and their relations. The corpus contains two types of reports, anamnesis and radiology. In both of them negation is a frequent phenomenon that needs to be treated for natural language processing purposes. The high IAA obtained suggests that the task is well defined. As expected, the agreement is higher for negation markers than for negated events, and higher in the anamnesis reports than in the radiology reports. As future work we plan to perform a detailed disagreement analysis in order to improve the guidelines for future annotation projects and to gain insight into the complexity of the task.

Acknowledgments

This work has been partially funded by the Andalusian Regional Govenment (Bidamir Project TIC-07629) and the Spanish Government (IPHealth Project TIN2013-47153-C3-2-R). RM is supported by the Netherlands Organization for Scientific Research (NWO) via the Spinoza-prize awarded to Piek Vossen (SPI 30-673, 2014-2019).

Many thanks to the annotators Carmen Cirilo and José Manuel Asencio.

References

Wendy W. Chapman, Will Bridewell, Paul Hanbury, Gregory Cooper, and Bruce G. Buchanan. 2001. A simple algorithm for identifying negated findings and diseases in discharge summaries. *Journal of biomedical informatics*, 35(5):301–310.

Roberto Costumero, Federico Lopez, Consuelo Gonzalo-Martín, Marta Millan, and Ernestina Menasalvas, 2014. *An Approach to Detect Negation on Medical Documents in Spanish*, pages 366–375. Springer International Publishing, Cham.

Viviana Cotik, Darío Filippo, and José Casta no. 2016. An approach for automatic classification of radiology reports in spanish. *Stud Health Technol Inform*, 216:634–638.

Lee R. Dice. 1945. Measures of the amount of ecologic association between species. *Ecology*, 26(3):297–302.

Salud María Jiménez-Zafra, Maite Martín, L. Alfonso Ureña Lopez, Toni Martí, and Mariona Taulé. 2016. Problematic cases in the annotation of negation in spanish. In *Proceedings of the Workshop on Extra-Propositional Aspects of Meaning in Computational Linguistics (ExProM)*, pages 42–48, Osaka, Japan, December. The COLING 2016 Organizing Committee.

Valentina Bartalesi Lenzi, Giovanni Moretti, and Rachele Sprugnoli. 2012. Cat: the celct annotation tool. In *In Proceedings of the Eigth International Conference on Language Resources and Evaluation (LREC 2012*, pages 333–338.

M. Antònia Martí, M. Teresa Martín-Valdivia, Mariona Taulé, Salud María Jiménez-Zafra, Montserrat Nofre, and Laia Marsó. 2016. La negación en español: análisis y tipología de patrones de negación. *Procesamiento del Lenguaje Natural*, 57:41–48.

Roser Morante and Eduardo Blanco. 2012. *SEM 2012 Shared Task: Resolving the scope and focus of negation. In *Proceedings of the First Joint Conference on Lexical and Computational Semantics*, pages 265–274, Stroudsburg, PA, USA. Association for Computational Linguistics.

Maite Oronoz, Koldo Gojenola, Alicia Pérez, Arantza Díaz de Ilarraza, and Arantza Casillas. 2015. On the creation of a clinical gold standard corpus in spanish. *J. of Biomedical Informatics*, 56(C):318–332, August.

Vanesa Stricker, Ignacio Iacobacci, and Viviana Coti. 2015. Negated findings detection in radiology reports in spanish: an adaptation of negex to spanish.

In *Proceedings of the IJCAI - Workshop on Replicability and Reproducibility in Natural Language Processing: adaptative methods, resources and software*, Buenos Aires, Argentina.

William Styler IV, Steven Bethard, Sean Finan, Martha Palmer, Sameer Pradhan, Piet de Groen, Brad Erickson, Timothy Miller, Chen Lin, Guergana Savova, and James Pustejovsky. 2014. Temporal annotation in the clinical domain. *Transactions of the Association for Computational Linguistics*, 2:143–154.

György Szarvas, Veronika Vincze, Richárd Farkas, and János Csirik. 2008. The bioscope corpus: annotation for negation, uncertainty and their scope in biomedical texts. In *Proceedings of the Workshop on Current Trends in Biomedical Natural Language Processing*, pages 38–45, Columbus, Ohio, June. Association for Computational Linguistics.

Maite Taboada, Caroline Anthony, and Kimberly Voll. 2006. Methods for creating semantic orientation dictionaries. In *Conference on Language Resources and Evaluation (LREC)*, pages 427–432.

Neural Networks for Negation Cue Detection in Chinese

Hangfeng He[1] **Federico Fancellu**[2] **Bonnie Webber**[2]
[1]School of Electronics Engineering and Computer Science, Peking University
[2]ILCC, School of Informatics, University of Edinburgh
hangfenghe@pku.edu.cn, f.fancellu@sms.ed.ac.uk, bonnie@inf.ed.ac.uk

Abstract

Negation cue detection involves identifying the span inherently expressing negation in a negative sentence. In Chinese, negative cue detection is complicated by morphological proprieties of the language. Previous work has shown that negative cue detection in Chinese can benefit from specific lexical and morphemic features, as well as cross-lingual information. We show here that they are not necessary: A bi-directional LSTM can perform equally well, with minimal feature engineering. In particular, the use of a character-based model allows us to capture characteristics of negation cues in Chinese using word-embedding information only. Not only does our model performs on par with previous work, further error analysis clarifies what problems remain to be addressed.

1 Introduction

Negation cue detection is the task of recognizing the tokens (words, multi-word units or morphemes) inherently expressing negation. For instance, the task in (1) is to detect the negation cue "不(not)", indicating that the clause as a whole is negative.

(1) 所有住客均表示不会追究酒店的这次管
理失职
(All of guests said that they would **not** investigate the dereliction of hotel.)

Previous work has addressed this task in English as a prerequisite for detecting negation scope (Fancellu et al., 2016; Cruz et al., 2015; Zou et al., 2013; Velldal et al., 2012; Zhu et al., 2010). But recently, the release of the CNeSp corpus (Zou et al., 2015) allows allows the task to be addressed in

Chinese as well. Detecting negation cues in Chinese texts is difficult because character cues can be homographs of or contained within words not expressing negation. For instance, "非常(very)" and "未来(future)" are not negation cues, while "非(not)" and "未(not)" are. Moreover, even expressions that contain a negation cue may not correspond to clause-level negation, because the overall meaning of the expression is positive. This can be observed in the expression "非要", roughly corresponding to the English expression "couldn't help but/had to" which contains the negation cue "非", but which carries a positive meaning where the action indeed take place, as in:

(2) ..., 到了后非要２００元, ...
...when we are arriving, they **had to** charge 200 yuan...

Finally, negation cues in Chinese are similar to English affixal cues (e.g. "*in*sufficient"), where they become integral part with the word they modify (e.g. 够("sufficient") → 不够("insufficient")). According to the CNeSp guidelines, both the negation affix and the root it attaches to are considered as part of the cue. The high combinatory power of negation affixes leads however to issues of data sparsity. This is particularly relevant in the context of the CNeSp corpus, given that about 12% of negation in the test set is not present in the training set (Zou et al., 2015, p. 660).

Specifically, using the CNeSp corpus, Zou et al. (2015) tried to automatically detect negation cues using a sequential classifier trained on a variety of features, including lexical (word n-grams), syntactic (PoS n-grams) and morphemic features (whether a character has appeared in training data as part of a cue). In addition, to address the problem of affixal negation cues producing tokens in the test set that did not appear in the training set, Chinese-to-English word-alignment was also

Proceedings of the Workshop Computational Semantics Beyond Events and Roles (SemBEaR), pages 59–63,
Valencia, Spain, April 4, 2017. ©2017 Association for Computational Linguistics

taken into account.

In contrast, the recent success of Neural Network models for negation scope detection (Fancellu et al., 2016) suggested investigating whether a character-based recurrent model can perform on par or better than this previous work. After describing our model in Section 2, we show in Section 3.3 that a character-level representation with no feature engineering is able to achieve similar *recall* as models that use word-alignment information, as well as other features, to tackle the problem of data sparsity. Compared to other sequence classifiers however, we show that neural networks tend to overpredict negation cues (thereby damaging *precision*) and suffer from insufficient training data.

2   The model

2.1   Input

We define a negative sentence as one that contains at least one negation cue. Given a sentence $ch = ch_1...ch_{|c|}$, we represent each character $ch_i \in ch$ as a d-dimensional character-embedding vector $ch_i^e \in \mathbb{R}^d$.

We define $E_{ch}^{v \times d}$ as the character-embedding matrix, where v is the vocabulary size. To represent a character along with its surrounding context in absence of any word segmentation, the input to the network is the concatenation of the current character ch_i with its neighboring characters in a fixed window size $2*m+1$. Our input instance will therefore be the concatenation of a given character plus its m proceeding and m succeeding characters as follows, $ch_{i-m}^e...ch_{i-1}^e; ch_i^e; ch_{i+1}^e...ch_{i+m}^e$.

2.2   BiLSTM Neural Network

The model we are going to use for this task is a Bi-LSTM model. Similar to RNNs, these models are able to leverage long-distance relations to predict whether a character is part of a negation cue or not. LSTM have however the advantage of better retaining information when backpropagating the error. On top of this, the bi-directionality allows to process the input left-to-right and viceversa, allowing for the entire sentential context to be taken in consideration at prediction time.

The inner computation of the LSTM network is as follows:

$$i_t = sigmoid(W_{ix}ch_t + W_{ih}h_{t-1} + b_i)$$

$$f_t = sigmoid(W_{fx}ch_t + W_{fh}h_{t-1} + b_f)$$

$$o_t = sigmoid(W_{ox}ch_t + W_{oh}h_{t-1} + b_o)$$

$$c_t = f_t*c_{t-1}+i_t*tanh(W_{cx}ch_t + W_{ch}h_{t-1}+b_c)$$

$$h_t = o_t * tanh(c_t)$$

where W are the weight matrices, i_t, f_t, o_t and c_t are the input, forget, output gate and cell state at position t, b the bias vector and h_t the hidden state representation at time t. The prediction of label y_t is computed as:

$$y_t = softmax(W_{hy}[h_t^{forw}; h_t^{back}] + b_y) \quad (1)$$

where W_{yh} is the output layer weight matrix and $[h_t^{forw}; h_t^{back}]$ the concatenation of the hidden states as computed during the forward and backward pass.

2.3   Transition Probability

Although the bi-LSTM keeps an internal memory of the inputs previously visited, the predictions made are independent from each other. For this reason, we introduce a new joint model $p(s|ch)$, defined as:

$$p(s|ch) = \prod_{i=1}^{n} p(s_i|s_{i-1}, ch)$$

The only functional change to the original LSTM model is the addition of a 4-parameter transition matrix to create the dependence on s_{i-1}, enabling the use of standard inference algorithms. This enables us to train the model end-to-end.

3   Experiments

3.1   Data

We use the Chinese Negation and Speculation (CNeSp) corpus (Zou et al., 2015) in our experiments. It is divided into three sub-corpora: Product reviews (below as *product*), Financial Articles (*financial*) and Computer-related Articles (*scientific*). (Corpus statistics appear in Table 1.) We first train and test on each corpus separately. We use a fixed 70%/15%/15% split of these in order to define a fixed development set for error analysis, but this setup precludes direct comparison to with (Zou et al., 2015), since they used 10-fold cross-validation. Nevertheless, we felt a data analysis was crucial to understanding these systems, and we wanted a clear distinction between test (for reporting results) and development (for analysis). For completeness, we also show results on training and testing when all corpora are joined together.

Models	Financial Article			Product Review			Scientific Literature			All		
	Precision	Recall	F1	Precision	Recall	F1	Precision	Recall	F1	Precision	Recall	F1
Baseline-Word	25.09	68.37	36.70	33.18	76.31	46.25	12.06	77.42	20.87	24.01	74.40	36.31
Baseline-Char	29.82	82.79	43.84	32.73	75.96	45.75	14.50	**93.55**	25.11	24.28	76.00	36.80
BiLSTM-*char*	61.94	71.16	66.23	78.93	**87.46**	**82.98**	**64.71**	35.48	**45.83**	69.08	**84.00**	75.81
+ Bigram	**65.15**	**73.02**	**68.86**	**79.05**	86.76	82.72	25.00	9.68	13.95	**71.70**	80.80	**75.98**
+ Transition	58.57	68.37	63.09	78.57	86.24	82.23	47.83	35.48	40.74	69.08	82.74	75.30

Table 2: Results on development set for each of the CNeSp subcorpora.

Models	Financial Article			Product Review			Scientific Literature			All		
	Precision	Recall	F1	Precision	Recall	F1	Precision	Recall	F1	Precision	Recall	F1
Zou et al. (2015)	**72.77**	67.02	**69.78**	81.94	89.23	85.43	**75.17**	78.91	**76.99**	-	-	-
Baseline-Word	24.76	66.52	36.09	30.93	72.47	43.36	12.32	**83.33**	21.46	22.13	71.68	33.82
Baseline-Char	28.66	**78.11**	41.94	33.41	78.75	46.91	12.32	**83.33**	21.46	23.68	77.89	36.32
BiLSTM-*char*	62.92	64.81	63.85	85.02	**91.99**	**88.37**	20.83	16.67	18.52	70.50	82.24	75.92
+ Bigram	63.41	66.95	65.14	**85.06**	91.29	88.07	7.14	3.33	4.55	**73.83**	80.25	76.90
+ Transition	63.08	70.39	66.53	84.56	89.72	87.07	14.29	10.00	11.76	72.49	**82.48**	**77.16**

Table 3: Results on test set for each of the CNeSp subcorpora.

	Sentence Number	Cue Number
Financial	6550	1461
Product	4969	3914
Scientific	4626	171

Table 1: Details of the three CNeSp subcorpora.

3.2 Settings

We experimented with three different settings:

- Character (*char.*): the input is a *single* character embedding, concatenated with the embeddings of its neighboring characters in a window size m.

- Character-bigram (*bigram*): the input is character *bigram* embedding obtained by the concatenation of the embeddings of two adjacent characters. We concatenate a bigram embedding with the embeddings of the neighboring character bigrams in a window size m. This reflects the observation that most negation cues are bigrams.

- Transition: a transition-based component is applied on top of the network (§2.3)

Our model is trained using stochastic gradient descent with L2 regularization. Learning rate is 0.01 with decay rate 0.95, m is 2 to yield a window size of 5; character embedding dimension and feature embedding dimension are both 100, discount κ in margin loss is 0.2, and the hyper parameter for the $L2$ is 0.000001.

Baseline. To understand the difficulty of cue detection, we designed two naive baselines based on a list of all negation cues contained in the training data: 1) *Baseline-Word*, where we classify as negation cue a character or a span of characters if it appears on the list, and 2) *Baseline-Char*, where we first segment the test sentence[1] and consider a word as cue if it contains any element on the list.

3.3 Results

Results on the development and test sets are shown in Tables 2 and 3 respectively. Both baselines achieves low precision compared to a higher recall which indicates that the challenge of this task lies in not overpredicting the negation cue span. A comparison of our models shows that character bigram information does not contribute to better performance, nor does the transition based component. Interpreting the poor performance on the *scientific* set is however difficult since there are only 171 cues in 4262 sentences, and only 12 in the 463 test sentences, a sample too small to draw any conclusion.

Table 3 also shows that neural network models with minimal feature engineering perform on par or better than the highly engineered sequential model used by Zou et al. (2015). Their higher recall show that they capture more negation cues, which is important, given that the approach does not use any cross-lingual alignment information to deal with test cues not seen during training. Finally, the results of the *scientific* test set show the same problem of small sample size as with the development set.

---

[1]For the segmentation we used the NLPIR toolkit: `https://github.com/NLPIR-team/NLPIR`

4 Error Analysis

4.1 Financial articles

Most of the errors in the *financial* sub-corpus are under-prediction errors. For instance, in the sentence (3), our model predicts "不景" as the negative cue, which is the under-prediction of "不景气".

(3) ...,受经济不景气影响,...
   (...,influenced by the economic **depression**,...)

In order to tackle this problem we carried out a small experiment where we post-process the results. We first used the NLPIR toolkit to automatically segment the sentence and if the detected cue is part of a word, then the whole word is considered as cue. The under-prediction error shows that the word segmentation information may be important in negation cue detection. When we apply this heuristic to the financial sub-corpus, we only noticed however only a small improvement across all measures as shown in Table 4.

	Precision	**Recall**	**F1**
Original	65.15	73.02	68.86
Post Process	**66.39**	**74.42**	**70.18**

Table 4: Difference between before and after post process in financial sub corpora

4.2 Product Review

Amongst the wrong predictions (121 in total) for the *Product Review* corpus, there are 61 sentences for which we predict more negative cues than gold one. These errors concern the most frequent negative cues such as "不(not)" and "没(not)". For instance, as shown in (4), our best model predicts "不(not)" as cue, which is different with the gold one.

(4) 房间设施一般，网速不仅慢还经常断网。
   (The room facilities are common and the network **not** only is slow but also often disconnect.)

These errors show that even expression that contain a negation cue may not correspond to clause-level negation. We also hypothesized that these wrong predictions are due to the fact that our model are not fed any explicit syntactic or semantic information regarding the context of a given character. Future work could explore the possibility of augmenting the input with extra information such as part of speech tags.

5 Conclusions and Future Work

In the present paper we addressed the problem of automatically detecting the negation cue in Chinese. In particular, we investigated whether character - based neural networks are able to achieve on par or better performance than previous highly engineered sequence classifiers. Results confirm that these models can be a valid alternative to previous ones, although still suffering from overgenerating the negation cue. In the process, we also found that one of the corpora we tested with might not be suitable to be used on its own, given the lack of enough instances.

Given the positive results obtained for Chinese, future work should focus in testing the method in English as well.

Acknowledgments

This project was funded in part by the European Union's Horizon 2020 research and innovation programme under grant agreement No 644402 (HimL). We also would like to thank the School of Electronic Engineering and Computer Science, Peking University for their support of Hangfeng He's internship at the University of Edinburgh.

The authors would like to thank the three anonymous reviewers for their comments.

References

Noa P. Cruz, Maite Taboada, and Ruslan Mitkov. 2015. A machine-learning approach to negation and speculation detection for sentiment analysis. *Journal of the Association for Information Science and Technology*.

Federico Fancellu, Adam Lopez, and Bonnie Webber. 2016. Neural networks for negation scope detection. In *Proceedings of the 54th Annual Meeting of the Association for Computational Linguistics*, volume 1, pages 495–504.

Erik Velldal, Lilja Øvrelid, Jonathon Read, and Stephan Oepen. 2012. Speculation and negation: Rules, rankers, and the role of syntax. *Computational linguistics*, 38(2):369–410.

Qiaoming Zhu, Junhui Li, Hongling Wang, and Guodong Zhou. 2010. A unified framework for scope learning via simplified shallow semantic parsing. In *Proceedings of the 2010 Conference on Empirical Methods in Natural Language Processing*, pages 714–724. Association for Computational Linguistics.

Bowei Zou, Guodong Zhou, and Qiaoming Zhu. 2013. Tree kernel-based negation and speculation scope detection with structured syntactic parse features. In *EMNLP*, pages 968–976.

Bowei Zou, Qiaoming Zhu, and Guodong Zhou. 2015. Negation and speculation identification in chinese language. In *ACL (1)*, pages 656–665.

An open-source tool for negation detection:
a maximum-margin approach

Martine Enger **Erik Velldal** **Lilja Øvrelid**

University of Oslo, Department of Informatics
{marenger,erikve,liljao}@ifi.uio.no

Abstract

This paper presents an open-source toolkit for negation detection. It identifies negation cues and their corresponding scope in either raw or parsed text using maximum-margin classification. The system design draws on best practice from the existing literature on negation detection, aiming for a simple and portable system that still achieves competitive performance. Pre-trained models and experimental results are provided for English.

1 Introduction

The task of negation detection has recently seen quite a bit of interest in the NLP community, in part spurred by the availability of annotated data and evaluation software introduced by the shared tasks at CoNLL 2010 (Farkas et al., 2010) and *SEM 2012 (Morante and Blanco, 2012). While many research-based systems have been developed, with the aim of exploring features and algorithms to advance the state-of-the-art in terms of performance (Morante and Daelemans, 2009; Read et al., 2012; Lapponi et al., 2012; Packard et al., 2014; Fancellu et al., 2016), many of them are difficult to employ in practice, due to layered architectures and many dependencies, and furthermore, most are simply not made publicly available in the first place.

In this paper, we present an open-source portable toolkit for automatic negation detection, with experimental results reported for English. The system is implemented in Python on top of PyStruct (Müller and Behnke, 2014), a library for structured prediction based on a maximum-margin approach. The system implements two stages of negation analysis, namely cue detection, which detects words that signal negation, such as *no, not*

and *un*fortunate, and scope resolution, which identifies the span of the sentence that is affected by the negation. Our negation toolkit builds on existing libraries that are actively maintained and easy to install, and the source[1] is made freely available (GPL). While we make pre-trained classifiers available (for English), users will also be able to train their own models.

The system design is based on best practices from previous work, in particular systems from the 2012 *SEM shared task. In particular, we adopt the practice of solving scope resolution as a sequence labeling task (Morante and Daelemans, 2009; Lapponi et al., 2012; White, 2012) based on syntactic features (Read et al., 2012; Lapponi et al., 2012; Packard et al., 2014). In contrast to many of the previous systems that have used constituency-based representations (Read et al., 2012; Packard et al., 2014), we base our syntactic features on dependency representations, similar to the approach of Lapponi et al. (2012). For cue detection, on the other hand, simply using surface-oriented lexical features have been shown to be sufficient, and we here largely build on the specific approach described by Read et al. (2012; Velldal et al. (2012), using a binary SVM classifier.

The main goal of this work is to arrive at a lean and light-weight system with minimal use of extra heuristics beyond machine learned models. While achieving the highest performance was not our main goal, the results are competitive with previously reported SoA results in the literature. Moreover, the system can be employed with both raw and parsed input data.

2 Experimental set-up

The Conan Doyle corpus The data set we use for training and testing is the Conan Doyle cor-

---

[1] https://github.com/marenger/negtool

Proceedings of the Workshop Computational Semantics Beyond Events and Roles (SemBEaR), pages 64–69,
Valencia, Spain, April 4, 2017. ©2017 Association for Computational Linguistics

pus (Morante and Daelemans, 2012) as used in the 2012 *SEM shared task (Morante and Blanco, 2012), based on a CoNLL-style format. While the shared task also included detection of events and focus, we only focus on cues and scopes in this work. We use the same splits for training, development testing and held-out evaluation as supplied for the shared task. Examples (1)-(2) below show two examples taken from the corpus, where negation cues are in bold and their scopes are underlined. In (1), the cue is the adverb *not*, whereas (2) provides an example of the affixal cue *un*.

(1) And yet it was **not** quite the last.

(2) Since we have been so **un**fortunate as to miss him and have no notion [...]

The Conan Doyle corpus provides phrase structure trees produced by the Charniak and Johnson (2005) parser, and we have used the Stanford Parser (Manning et al., 2014) to convert these to Stanford basic dependency representations (de Marneffe et al., 2014) prior to training.

Evaluation We use the evaluation script of the 2012 *SEM shared task (Morante and Blanco, 2012) for measuring precision, recall and F-score. For scopes, it provides two different measures; *token-level* and *scope-level*. For the token-level measure the evaluation is defined similarly as for cues, simply checking whether each token in the scope sequence is correctly labeled. For scopes on the other hand, a true positive requires both the entire scope sequence and cue to be correct.

Note that for the held-out results, our system is trained on both the development and training data combined.

System comparison In addition to providing baseline results for both cues and scopes, we also include the results for the UiO$_2$ system of Lapponi et al. (2012) from the *SEM shared task. Achieving the best results for both cue and scope resolution in the open track, it has guided much of the design of the current system. The cue classification component of UiO$_2$ was the same as for UiO$_1$ (run 1) (Read et al., 2012) – the system that was ranked first in the shared task overall (though not for cue detection in isolation).

Maximum-margin learning for cues and scopes While cue detection is here approached as a token-wise classification problem and scope resolution as sequence classification, they are both modeled using a maximum-margin approach. Cue detection is solved using a binary Support Vector Machine (SVM) classifier (Vapnik, 1995). As is fairly common, scope resolution is solved as a sequence labeling task, applying a discriminative linear-chain Conditional Random Fields (CRF) model.However, in a conventional CRF, the parameters are learned through maximum likelihood estimation. In PyStruct on the other hand, the parameters are estimated through maximum-margin learning based on SVMs, resulting in what may be called a maximum-margin CRF.

System requirements The input given to the system can either be raw running text or parsed data in the CoNLL-X format (Buchholz and Marsi, 2006). If the user inputs raw text, we need to tokenize, tag and parse the text before we can classify the sentences. Because our training data uses PTB PoS-tags and Stanford dependencies (following conversion), we need a pipeline providing the same standard, and hence use the CoreNLP tool (Manning et al., 2014). Beyond Python 2.7 or newer, the negation tool has the following dependencies: scikit-learn, PyStruct, NumPy, and NetworkX (in addition to CoreNLP unless pre-parsed input is provided).

3 Cue identification

The task of cue detection is to identify potential cue words and determine whether they function as negation cues in the given context. Cue detection is here solved using a binary SVM classifier and follows the filtering approach described by Velldal (2011) and Read et al. (2012) which means that not all words in the input text are presented to the classifier. Instead we extract a lexicon of known single-word cues from the training data and only attempt to disambiguate these (any other word will always be labeled as a non-cue). Additionally, a separate lexicon of affixal cues is also automatically extracted, consisting of affixes seen in the training data, viz. the prefixes {*dis, im, in, ir, un*}, the infix *less*, and the suffix *less*. The cue classifier is presented with any words that match either of these at the respective positions, e.g. words that have a prefix that matches any of the prefixes, e.g. *im*patient and *im*age.

In theory, this way of restricting the problem to a closed class of candidates will put a cap on the upper bound of recall. In practice, Velldal (2011) found that it could still outperform full

	Development			Held-out		
	P	**R**	**F1**	**P**	**R**	**F1**
Baseline	90.68	84.39	87.42	87.10	92.05	89.51
UiO$_2$	93.75	95.38	94.56	89.17	93.56	91.31
System	91.67	95.38	93.49	90.15	93.56	91.82

Table 1: Cue classification

word-by-word classification where all words are considered. It simplifies the problem in that much fewer instances need to be considered, thereby also greatly reducing the feature space, and also gives much more balanced classes.

Multi-word cues, like '*by no means*' or '*neither...nor*', are handled by a few simple post-processing rules, simply checking whether a given cue word forms part of a multi-word cue in the given context. Using a small stop-list, some forms like *by* and *means* are excluded from the list of candidate cue words considered by the classifier.

As a baseline we use a majority class classifier, labeling each word by its most frequent label in the training data. Table 1 shows that this simple baseline is already quite strong: With an F1 of 89.51 on the held-out data it outperforms 4 of the 12 systems submitted for the *SEM shared task.

The feature configuration of the cue classifier is based on a grid search towards the development set mostly based on features previously described by Read et al. (2012; Velldal et al. (2012), tuning the SVM C parameter separately for each configuration. The final model uses the following features for each token to be classified: The word form, PoS and lemma of the token, as well as lemmas $\pm$ 1 position. For candidates of affixal cues we additionally extract the affix itself and character n-grams up to n=5 of the base-form that the affix attaches to (extracted from both the beginning and the end of the form). In terms of PyStruct configuration we use its BinaryClf model with the NSlackSSVM estimator, with the C regularization parameter set to 0.2.

The results are shown in Table 1. We see that there is a slight drop in F1-score when moving from the development set to the held-out set (from 93.49 to 91.82). Compared to UiO$_2$, we see that while the recall of the two systems are identical, the precision of our system is almost 1 percentage point higher. Overall, our cue classifier would have ranked third in the *SEM 2012 shared task.

4 Scope resolution

Our approach to scope resolution largely follows that of the UiO$_2$ system of Lapponi et al. (2012) from the *SEM shared task, both in terms of the choice of machine learning algorithm, the internal data representation and the set of features used to represent the negation scopes. Like them, we model scope resolution as a sequence labeling task, making use of both lexical and syntactic information regarding the context of a negation cue. Just as for the cue classifier, we performed extensive tuning towards the development set for the maximum-margin CRF scope model – experimenting with different features, sequence labels, and hyper-parameters – finally arriving at the following configuration:

Surface features: The word form, lemma ($\pm$ 1 position), and PoS ($\pm$ 1 position)

Cue features: Cue type, left/right cue distance, and cue PoS.

Dependency features: Directed dependency distance, dependency graph path.

Note that the directed dependency path is the shortest path from the head of the cue to the current token. Internally, we employ the following label set to represent scopes: I, O, B, and C (Inside, Outside, Beginning, and Cue). Note that the only post-processing performed after the CRF is ensuring that the cue is always out-of-scope and that the base of an affixal cue is always in-scope. In terms of PyStruct configuration we use its chain CRF model, with the FrankWolfeSSVM estimator, with the C regularization parameter set to 0.1.

The results are presented in Table 2. As for the cue results in Table 1 we here too report the performance of the UiO$_2$ system as a point of reference. In addition, we also include results for a baseline corresponding to labeling the entire sentence as in-scope if it contains a (gold) negation cue. While this section focuses on scope prediction performance in isolation using gold cues, Section 5 discusses the end-to-end results with scope resolution for predicted cues.

We see that the baseline scores are much lower on the evaluation set than the development set, with the scope-level F-score decreasing from 32.03% on development to 19.24% on the evaluation set. However, our maximum-margin scope classifier appears to be robust to this gap, and its

| | Development | | | | | | Held-out | | | | | |
| | Scope-level | | | Token-level | | | Scope-level | | | Token-level | | |
	P	R	F1	P	R	F1	P	R	F1	P	R	F1
Baseline (gold cues)	86.84	19.64	32.03	45.00	97.55	61.59	66.67	11.24	19.24	38.54	98.01	55.32
UiO_2 (gold cues)	100.00	66.67	80.00	90.64	81.36	85.75	-	-	-	-	-	-
System (gold cues)	100.00	63.10	77.38	90.80	82.05	86.20	98.75	63.45	77.26	91.47	81.39	86.14
UiO_2	-	-	-	-	-	-	85.71	62.65	72.39	86.03	81.55	83.73
System	88.14	61.90	72.73	85.24	80.56	82.83	85.00	61.45	71.33	85.49	80.28	82.80

Table 2: Scope resolution, for both gold and predicted cues.

performance remains largely unchanged across the two test sets, with only a 0.12 percentage points decrease in F-score for the scope-level and 0.06 on the token-level.

Turning to the development results of the scope CRF model of UiO_2 (on gold cues), we find that the scores are slightly higher than ours with respect to the scope-level, but slightly lower for the token-level. For the held-out evaluation data on the other hand, UiO_2 scope results for gold cues were not reported, like for most of the other *SEM competition systems, unfortunately. However, the system description of the UiO_1 system (Read et al., 2012) – implementing a hybrid approach combining manually defined rules and SVM-based ranking of constituent (sub-)trees – reports scope-level scores for gold cues on both the development and evaluation data. The same holds for the system of Packard et al. (2014), which combines the UiO_1 system with an additional layer of manually defined rules over Minimal Recursion Semantics structures created by an HPSG parser. For both of these systems we can observe a larger drop in F1 when moving from the development data to the evaluation data, with the UiO_1/MRS-combination dropping from 82.5 to 78.7, and with the UiO_1 system[2] on its own dropping from 82.52 to 77.26 (compared to the drop from 77.38 to 77.26 in the case of our system). Regardless of the causes for these differences, it at least appears that our purely CRF-based system, with the tuning of the C parameter for the underlying maximum-margin model, does not suffer any overfitting effects. At the same time, we see that the combined system of Packard et al. (2014) achieves the highest absolute scores, and we return to this point when discussing end-to-end results below. Fi-

nally, note that Fancellu et al. (2016) report scope results on the *SEM evaluation data (gold cues only) for a suite of different classifiers based on a bi-directional LSTM, with the best configuration obtaining a scope-level F-score of 77.77. In sum, we observe two things; (i) our scope classifier achieves competetive performance, and (ii) despite the large differences in terms of types of approaches and architectures for the various scope systems considered here, there are not large differences in terms of performance.

4.1 Error analysis

We performed an error analysis of our scope resolution predictions over the development data using gold cues. The analysis shows that our system struggles with discontinuous scopes, as in (3):

(3) It was **not**, I must confess, a very alluring prospect.

This is not surprising, seeing that several of the top performing systems implements dedicated post-processing modules for dealing with discontinuous scopes. The error analysis also reveals other types of recurring scope errors, including sentences that contains multiple negation cues with overlapping scopes (gold-standard). Moreover, we also observed that many of the sentences that are counted as false negatives with respect to the strict exact match scope-level measure often just have a single token that is incorrectly labeled, meaning that the overall scope is very close to being correct. This is reflected in the fact that the token-level F-score is roughly 10 percentage points higher than the scope-level F-score.

5 End-to-end results

As expected, the scope scores drop when moving from gold to predicted cues, mostly in terms of precision, which for the scope-level on the development set was 100% with gold cues but 88.14%

---

[2]We here report results for 'run II' of UiO_1 as submitted for the *SEM 2012 shared task, since this version of the system was optimized towards the development set just like in our set-up, while 'run I' was optimized by cross-validation on the training and development data combined.

with predicted cues. Errors from the cue classifier propagates to the scope classifier which will attempt to predict scopes for false positive cues. Our end-to-end results would have ranked fourth in the *SEM 2012 shared task with respect to the relevant subtasks.

In the time passed since the shared task, the best published results on the evaluation data appears to be for the system of Packard et al. (2014). Building on top of the UiO_1 system, it obtains a scope-level F1 of 73.1. Depending on the goal, however, F-score in isolation is not the only relevant dimension for system comparisons. The goal of the current work is to create a practically usable tool. For an applied and practical setting, it is also relevant to consider other system properties, like the number of dependencies, platform compatibility, the degree of manual engineering – which can in turn affect how easy it will be to re-train the system on new data or porting the system to cope with other phenomena, the amount of required linguistic pre-processing, and so on. In the system of Packard et al. (2014), the underlying UiO_1 system (Read et al., 2012) is used for cue prediction and as a second source for scope-prediction. While UiO_1 itself is already a highly engineered system – combining manually defined heuristics and statistical ranking of constituent sub-trees – Packard et al. (2014) add a second layer of both (HPSG) parsing and rules (over MRS representations). In sum, the 1.77 point increase in F1 compared to the current system comes at the cost of substantially increased complexity. Importantly though, the full system pipeline is also not publicly available.[3]

For the BiLSTM scope classifier of Fancellu et al. (2016) discussed in Section 4, no results are reported for cue classification, and scope results are only reported for gold cues.[4] Although the code for the BiLSTM scope model is made available, end-to-end results can not be compared without a cue classifier.

---

[3] The paper of Packard et al. (2014) points to code for replicating the reported experiments, but this only includes support for computing the final layer of 'MRS crawling'. The system of Packard et al. (2014) also relies on cue- and scope predictions from the so-called UiO_1 system of Read et al. (2012), however, and these predictions are only provided in the form of pre-computed system output for the *SEM shared task data; the underlying UiO_1 system is not itself available.

[4] In the system comparison reported by Fancellu et al. (2016), the results of the *SEM shared task competition systems are based on predicted cues while the results of Packard et al. (2014) and Fancellu et al. (2016) are for gold cues, making them not comparable.

6 Future work

One possible improvement of the system would be to extend the scope resolution with post-processing heuristics for targeting discontinuous scopes. The best overall system in the *SEM shared task implemented this (Read et al., 2012), and while the rules themselves require some linguistic understanding, they would be fairly straightforward to implement. There are also certain multi-word cues occurring in the data set that are not covered by the heuristics currently implemented in the system.

Beyond the multi-word cue heuristics, our implementation is abstract in the sense that it is not hard-coded for negation, instead relying on models to be learned automatically from any data using a CoNLL style format similar to that of the *SEM shared task. Importantly, this means that the tool could be trained for other similar tasks, such as speculation detection, as long as cues and scopes are marked. One interesting direction here would be to convert the annotations of the BioScope corpus (Vincze et al., 2008) to the format used by the Conan Doyle corpus. This would allow training of both speculation and negation detection models for biomedical data, and also to test cross-domain effects. Such a conversion is not entirely trivial, however, as the resources differ not merely in terms of format but also the underlying annotation rules. Developing such a mapping could greatly benefit this research field, also making it possible to use data from different domains.

7 Conclusion

This paper has presented an open-source tool for detecting negation cues and their in-sentence scopes. Despite the substantial amount of previous work on negation detection, this has not left much in terms of reusable tools. The presented toolkit mostly relies on machine-learned models, based on a maximum-margin approach. While pre-trained models for English are distributed along with the code, users can also train their own models. In terms of learning frameworks and features, the system design draws on best practice from the existing literature on negation detection, aiming for a simple and portable system that still achieves competitive performance. For future work we plan to also use the tool for training and testing models for speculation detection.

References

Sabine Buchholz and Erwin Marsi. 2006. CoNLL-X shared task on Multilingual Dependency Parsing. In *Proceedings of the Tenth Conference on Computational Natural Language Learning*, pages 149–164, New York, USA.

Eugene Charniak and Mark Johnson. 2005. Coarse-to-fine n-best parsing and maxent discriminative reranking. In *Proceedings of the 43rd Annual Meeting of the Association for Computational Linguistics*, pages 173–180, Ann Arbor, MI, USA.

Marie-Catherine de Marneffe, Timothy Dozat, Natalia Silveira, Katri Haverinen, Filip Ginter, Joakim Nivre, and Christopher D. Manning. 2014. Universal Stanford dependencies. A cross-linguistic typology. In *Proceedings of the International Conference on Language Resources and Evaluation*, pages 4585–4592, Reykjavik, Iceland.

Federico Fancellu, Adam Lopez, and Bonnie Weber. 2016. Neural Networks for Negation Scope Detection. In *Proceedings of The 54th Annual Meeting of the Association for Computational Linguistics*, pages 495–504, Berlin, Germany.

Richard Farkas, Veronika Vincze, Gyorgy Mora, Janos Csirik, and Gyrgy Szarvas. 2010. The CoNLL 2010 Shared Task: Learning to detect hedges and their scope in natural language text. In *Proceedings of the 14th Conference on Natural Language Learning*, pages 1–12, Uppsala, Sweden.

Emanuele Lapponi, Erik Velldal, Lilja Øvrelid, and Jonathon Read. 2012. UiO_2: Sequence-Labeling Negation Using Dependency Features. In *Proceedings of the First Joint Conference on Lexical and Computational Semantics (*SEM)*, pages 319–327, Montreal, Canada.

Christopher D. Manning, Mihai Surdeanu, John Bauer, Jenny Finkel, Steven J. Bethard, and David McClosky. 2014. The Stanford CoreNLP natural language processing toolkit. In *Proceedings of 52nd Annual Meeting of the Association for Computational Linguistics: System Demonstrations*, pages 55–60, Baltimore, Maryland, USA.

Roser Morante and Eduardo Blanco. 2012. *SEM 2012 Shared Task: Resolving the Scope and Focus of Negation. In *Proceedings of the First Joint Conference on Lexical and Computational Semantics (*SEM)*, pages 265–274, Montreal, Canada. Association for Computational Linguistic.

Roser Morante and Walter Daelemans. 2009. A metalearning approach to processing the scope of negation. In *Proceesings of the Thirteenth Conference on Computational Natural Language Learning*, pages 21–29, Boulder, Colorado, USA.

Roser Morante and Walter Daelemans. 2012. ConanDoyle-neg: Annotation of negation in Conan Doyle stories. In *Proceedings of the First Joint Conference on Lexical and Computational Semantics (*SEM)*, pages 1563–1568, Montreal, Canada.

Andreas C. Müller and Sven Behnke. 2014. PyStruct - Learning Structured Prediction in Python. *Journal of Machine Learning Research*, 15:2055–2060.

Woodley Packard, Emily M. Bender, Jonathon Read, Stephan Oepen, and Rebecca Dridan. 2014. Simple Negation Scope Resolution through Deep Parsing: A Semantic Solution to a Semantic Problem. In *Proceedings of the 52nd Annual Meeting of the Association for Computational Linguistics*, pages 69–78, Baltimore, USA.

Jonathon Read, Erik Velldal, Lilja Øvrelid, and Stephan Oepen. 2012. UiO_1: Constituent-Based Discriminative Ranking for Negation Resolution. In *Proceedings of the First Joint Conference on Lexical and Computational Semantics (*SEM)*, pages 310–318, Montreal, Canada.

Vladimir N. Vapnik. 1995. The Nature of Statistical Learning Theory. *Springer-Verlag*.

Erik Velldal, Lilja Øvrelid, Jonathon Read, and Stephan Oepen. 2012. Speculation and negation: Rules, rankers and the role of syntax. *Computational Linguistics*, 38:369–410.

Erik Velldal. 2011. Predicting speculation: A simple disambiguation approach to hedge detection in biomedical literature. *Journal of Biomedical Semantics*, 2(5).

Veronika Vincze, Gyrgy Szarvas, Richrd Farkas, Gyrgy Mra, and Jnos Csirik. 2008. The BioScope corpus: biomedical texts annotated for uncertainty, negation and their scopes. *BMC Bioinformatics*, 9(11).

James Paul White. 2012. UWashington: Negation Resolution using Machine Learning Methods. In *Proceedings of the First Joint Conference on Lexical and Computational Semantics (*SEM)*, pages 335–339, Montreal, Canada.

Association for Computational Linguistics
209 N. Eighth Street
Stroudsburg, Pennsylvania 18360

ISBN 978-1-5108-3869-7

9 781510 838697